Folens
Geography in Action 6

Author:
John Corn

Acknowledgements

© 2006 Folens Limited, on behalf of the author.

United Kingdom: Folens Publishers, Apex Business Centre, Boscombe Road, Dunstable, LU5 4RL.
Email: folens@folens.com

Ireland: Folens Publishers, Greenhills Road, Tallaght, Dublin 24.
Email: info@folens.ie

Poland: JUKA, ul. Renesansowa 38, Warsaw 01-905.

Folens allows photocopying of pages marked 'copiable page' for educational use, providing that this use is within the confines of the purchasing institution. Copiable pages should not be declared in any return in respect of any photocopying licence.

Folens publications are protected by international copyright laws. All rights are reserved. The copyright of all materials in this publication, except where otherwise stated, remains the property of the publisher and author. No part of this publication may be reproduced, stored in a retrieval system, or transmitted, in any form or by any means, for whatever purpose, without the written permission of Folens Limited.

John Corn hereby asserts his moral right to be identified as the author of this work in accordance with the Copyright, Designs and Patents Act 1988.

Commissioning editor: Zoë Nichols   Editor: Joanne Mitchell   Layout artist: Suzanne Ward

Illustrations: Alan Baker pp6, 8, 9, 11, 12, 13, 16, 19, 20, 23, 25, 29, 33 (postcards), 34, 48, 49, 60 (middle left and bottom right), 70; Celia Hart pp7, 15, 26, 39, 60 (top left and middle right), 63 (bottom), 72; Catherine Ward pp21, 28, 30, 31, 33 (middle), 37, 38, 41, 43, 44, 46, 51, 52, 53, 55, 56, 57, 59, 63 (top and middle), 64, 65, 67, 68, 69, 73, 74, 75, 77, 78.

Cover design: Philippa Jarvis   Cover image: Ashley Cooper/CORBIS

First published 2006 by Folens Limited.

Every effort has been made to contact copyright holders of material used in this publication. If any copyright holder has been overlooked, we should be pleased to make any necessary arrangements.

British Library Cataloguing in Publication Data. A catalogue record for this publication is available from the British Library.

ISBN 1 84303 804 8

Contents

Introduction	4
THE MOUNTAIN ENVIRONMENT	5–31
Mountains and Mountain Ranges	5
M1 Climate zones	6
M2 Mountain areas	7
M3 High spots	8
M4 Ranging mountains	9
Mountain Environments	10
M5 Artefacts (1)	11
M6 Artefacts (2)	12
M7 Artefacts (3)	13
Mountains Around the World	14
M8 Climate data	15
M9 White walls	16
M10 Mount Kilimanjaro	17
Whatever the Weather	18
M11 All seasons holidays	19
M12 Black run	20
M13 Lakes and mountains	21
The Highest Junkyard in the World	22
M14 The world's highest junkyard	23
M15 Mixed blessing	24
M16 Quiet village – crowded resort	25
M17 Sign of the times	26
Holidays in the Mountains	27
M18 Under canvas	28
M19 Head for the hills	29
M20 Mountain trek (1)	30
M21 Mountain trek (2)	31
INVESTIGATING COASTS	32–61
Changing Coastlines	32
C1 Coast to coast	33
C2 Breakers	34
C3 Deposition	35
Coastal Erosion	36
C4 Mapping the coast	37
C5 Cliff attack	38
C6 Holbeck Hall Hotel	39
Beaches	40
C7 On the beach	41
C8 Longshore drift	42
C9 Dune	43
C10 Spurn Head	44

Visiting the Coast	45
C11 Beside the seaside	46
C12 Activity holidays	47
C13 Birdwatching	48
C14 Rock-climbing	49
Features and Land Uses Around the Coast	50
C15 Field sketch	51
C16 Exploring coastlines	52
C17 Coastliners	53
Managing the Coast	54
C18 Coastal defence	55
C19 Shifting sands	56
C20 Holding back the tide	57
Developing the Coast	58
C21 Truffles Hotel	59
C22 For or against?	60
C23 Labels	61
INVESTIGATING RIVERS	62–80
Different Kinds of Rain	62
R1 Every time it rains	63
R2 Rainfall map	64
R3 Water cycle	65
Water Around the School	66
R4 Micro-climate	67
R5 Water, water everywhere	68
R6 Map making	69
R7 Measuring puddles	70
Rivers in the Landscape	71
R8 Go with the flow	72
R9 Information stream (1)	73
R10 Information stream (2)	74
R11 Mapping streams	75
Rivers Near and Far	76
R12 River file	77
R13 Flood	78
R14 World rivers (1)	79
R15 World rivers (2)	80

Introduction

Folens Geography in Action meets the requirements for the National Curriculum in England and Wales, and is compatible with the schemes of work published in England by the Qualifications and Curriculum Authority (QCA). It will work best when combined with a range of geographical resources such as Ordnance Survey maps, road atlases, globes, wall maps, books, photographs and aerial photographs. In many units, fieldwork is an important component.

Aims of Folens Geography in Action

The overall aim of the book is that children should develop knowledge and understanding of different places and the processes that have shaped the landscape. They are encouraged to use appropriate geographical vocabulary, secondary source material and information gained from fieldwork to discover how people are affected by the environment they live in and how they can change it.

The aim of individual activities is to provide opportunities for the children to engage with the subject matter and process it in different ways, such as by drawing and interpreting maps, labelling diagrams and writing descriptions and explanations. Children are encouraged to work individually, in pairs or small groups so that during certain activities they can work together, listen to others' views and make individual and collective decisions.

The Structure of Folens Geography in Action

The book is divided into three units, each covering a geography topic suitable for Year 6, as defined by the schemes of work. Each unit contains a term's work; it is expected that two of the units will be covered over the course of a year.

The Mountain Environment encourages the children to study, through research, places that share a similar physical environment. The unit looks at the distribution, character and weather in mountain environments and requires the children to consider how these fragile environments can be protected from the affects of tourism.

Investigating Coasts and **Investigating Rivers** are again concerned with the physical environment and contain an element of fieldwork. Children will benefit greatly from the opportunity to study physical processes at first-hand, but often fieldwork is not practicable due not least to the pressures of time and distance. The material contained within the units looks at the effects of water in the landscape and the landforms and issues that the interactions produce. **Investigating Coasts** could be studied as an alternative to **Investigating Rivers**.

The units are further divided into sub-topics, each starting with a teachers' page. The teachers' page contains notes to explain and provide background for the activity sheets which follow.

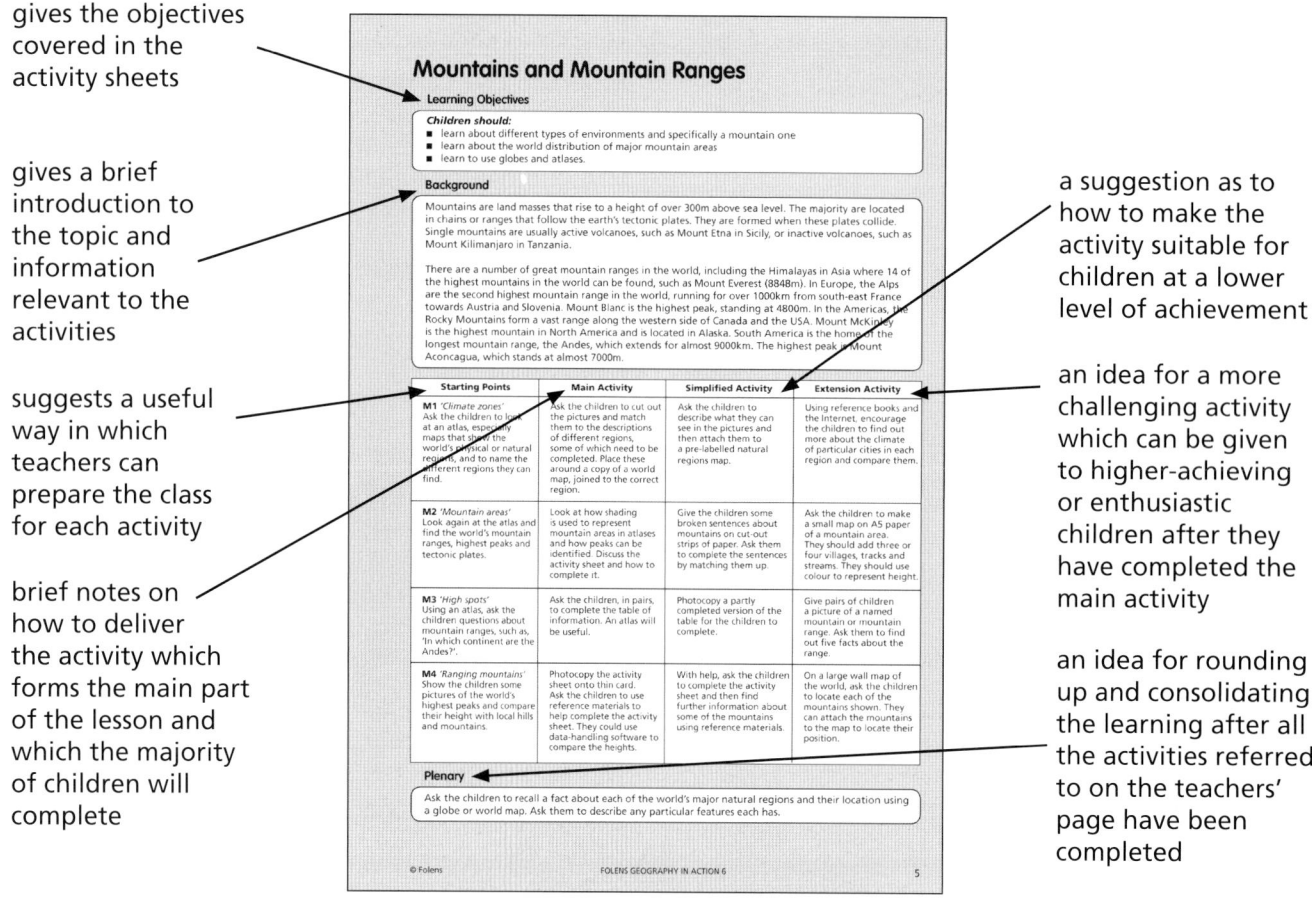

---

gives the objectives covered in the activity sheets

gives a brief introduction to the topic and information relevant to the activities

suggests a useful way in which teachers can prepare the class for each activity

brief notes on how to deliver the activity which forms the main part of the lesson and which the majority of children will complete

a suggestion as to how to make the activity suitable for children at a lower level of achievement

an idea for a more challenging activity which can be given to higher-achieving or enthusiastic children after they have completed the main activity

an idea for rounding up and consolidating the learning after all the activities referred to on the teachers' page have been completed

Mountains and Mountain Ranges

Learning Objectives

Children should:
- learn about different types of environments and specifically a mountain one
- learn about the world distribution of major mountain areas
- learn to use globes and atlases.

Background

Mountains are land masses that rise to a height of over 300m above sea level. The majority are located in chains or ranges that follow the earth's tectonic plates. They are formed when these plates collide. Single mountains are usually active volcanoes, such as Mount Etna in Sicily, or inactive volcanoes, such as Mount Kilimanjaro in Tanzania.

There are a number of great mountain ranges in the world, including the Himalayas in Asia where 14 of the highest mountains in the world can be found, such as Mount Everest (8848m). In Europe, the Alps are the second highest mountain range in the world, running for over 1000km from south-east France towards Austria and Slovenia. Mount Blanc is the highest peak, standing at 4800m. In the Americas, the Rocky Mountains form a vast range along the western side of Canada and the USA. Mount McKinley is the highest mountain in North America and is located in Alaska. South America is the home of the longest mountain range, the Andes, which extends for almost 9000km. The highest peak is Mount Aconcagua, which stands at almost 7000m.

Starting Points	Main Activity	Simplified Activity	Extension Activity
M1 *'Climate zones'* Ask the children to look at an atlas, especially maps that show the world's physical or natural regions, and to name the different regions they can find.	Ask the children to cut out the pictures and match them to the descriptions of different regions, some of which need to be completed. Place these around a copy of a world map, joined to the correct region.	Ask the children to describe what they can see in the pictures and then attach them to a pre-labelled natural regions map.	Using reference books and the Internet, encourage the children to find out more about the climate of particular cities in each region and compare them.
M2 *'Mountain areas'* Look again at the atlas and find the world's mountain ranges, highest peaks and tectonic plates.	Look at how shading is used to represent mountain areas in atlases and how peaks can be identified. Discuss the activity sheet and how to complete it.	Give the children some broken sentences about mountains on cut-out strips of paper. Ask them to complete the sentences by matching them up.	Ask the children to make a small map on A5 paper of a mountain area. They should add three or four villages, tracks and streams. They should use colour to represent height.
M3 *'High spots'* Using an atlas, ask the children questions about mountain ranges, such as, 'In which continent are the Andes?'.	Ask the children, in pairs, to complete the table of information. An atlas will be useful.	Photocopy a partly completed version of the table for the children to complete.	Give pairs of children a picture of a named mountain or mountain range. Ask them to find out five facts about the range.
M4 *'Ranging mountains'* Show the children some pictures of the world's highest peaks and compare their height with local hills and mountains.	Photocopy the activity sheet onto thin card. Ask the children to use reference materials to help complete the activity sheet. They could use data-handling software to compare the heights.	With help, ask the children to complete the activity sheet and then find further information about some of the mountains using reference materials.	On a large wall map of the world, ask the children to locate each of the mountains shown. They can attach the mountains to the map to locate their position.

Plenary

Ask the children to recall a fact about each of the world's major natural regions and their location using a globe or world map. Ask them to describe any particular features each has.

Climate zones

- Complete the empty boxes with descriptions of the particular climate regions (polar, mountain, rainforest, desert). Cut out the pictures and the descriptions, match them up and attach them to a map of the world, joining them to each climate zone.

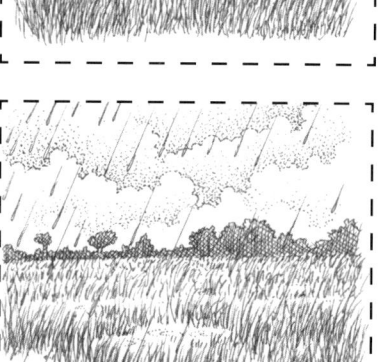

Polar –

Rainforest –

Cold forest – long, cold winters; warm, brief summers; extensive forests.

Savanna – wet and dry seasons; warm to hot all year round; tall grasslands.

Temperate – warm summers; cool winters; rainfall all year round; intensive farming.

Desert –

Mediterranean – hot, dry summers; mild, wet winters; intensive farming.

Monsoon – dry and hot for much of the year; intense rainfall for about three months of the year.

Mountain –

Mountain areas

- Label and colour the world's major mountain areas using an atlas and the words below.

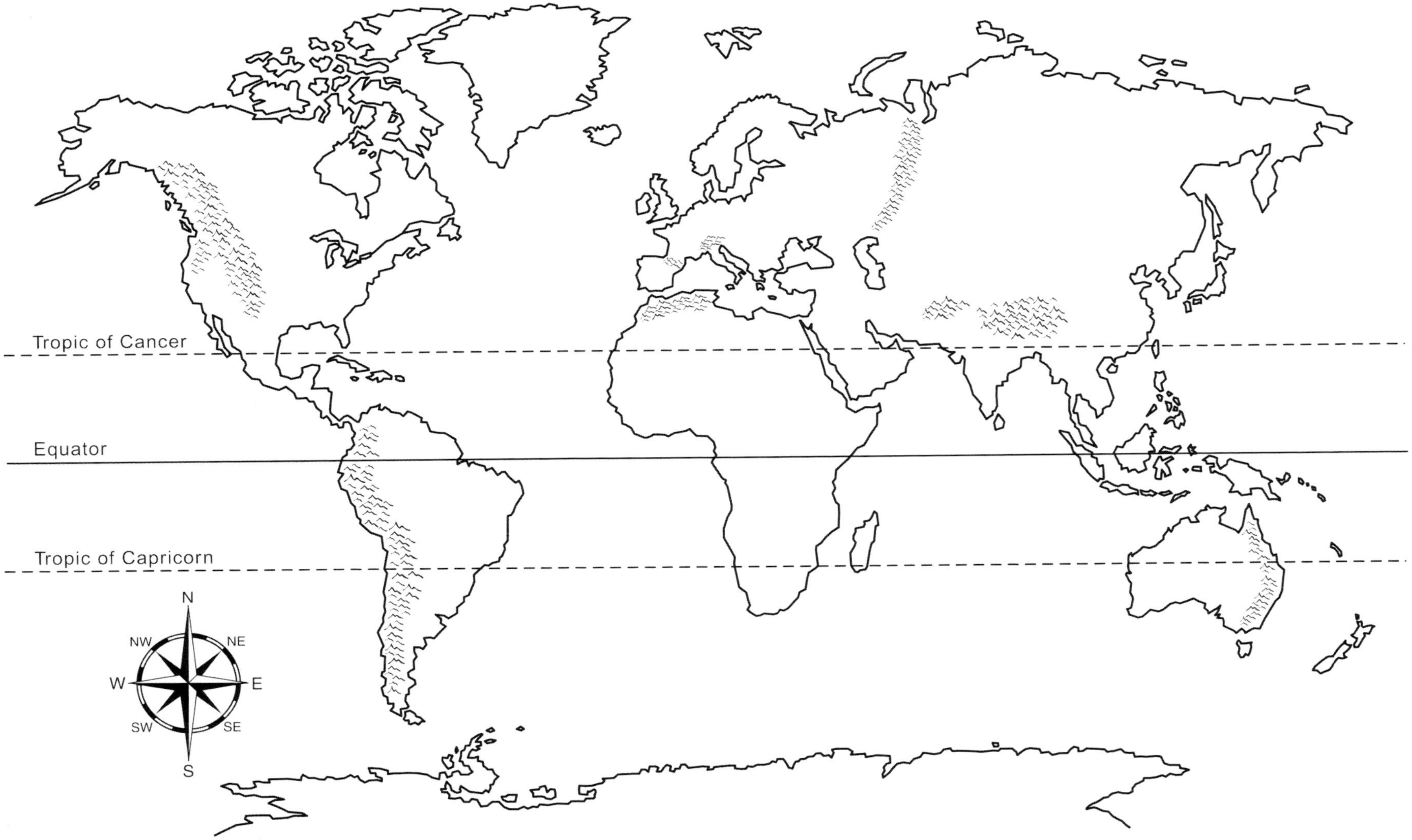

Tropic of Cancer

Equator

Tropic of Capricorn

Rockies   Alps   Andes   Himalayas   Great Divide   Atlas   Lake District

High spots

- Use an atlas to help you to complete the chart below.

	Rocky Mountains	Andes	Alps	Himalayas	Atlas Mountains	Great Divide	Lake District
Continent found in							
Countries							
Length of range (km)							
Highest peak (m)							
Distance from London (km)							
Direction from London							

Ranging mountains

M4

- Cut out, then fold so that the mountains stand up. Rank them in order of height. Draw five more mountains, add details from reference books and put these in order.

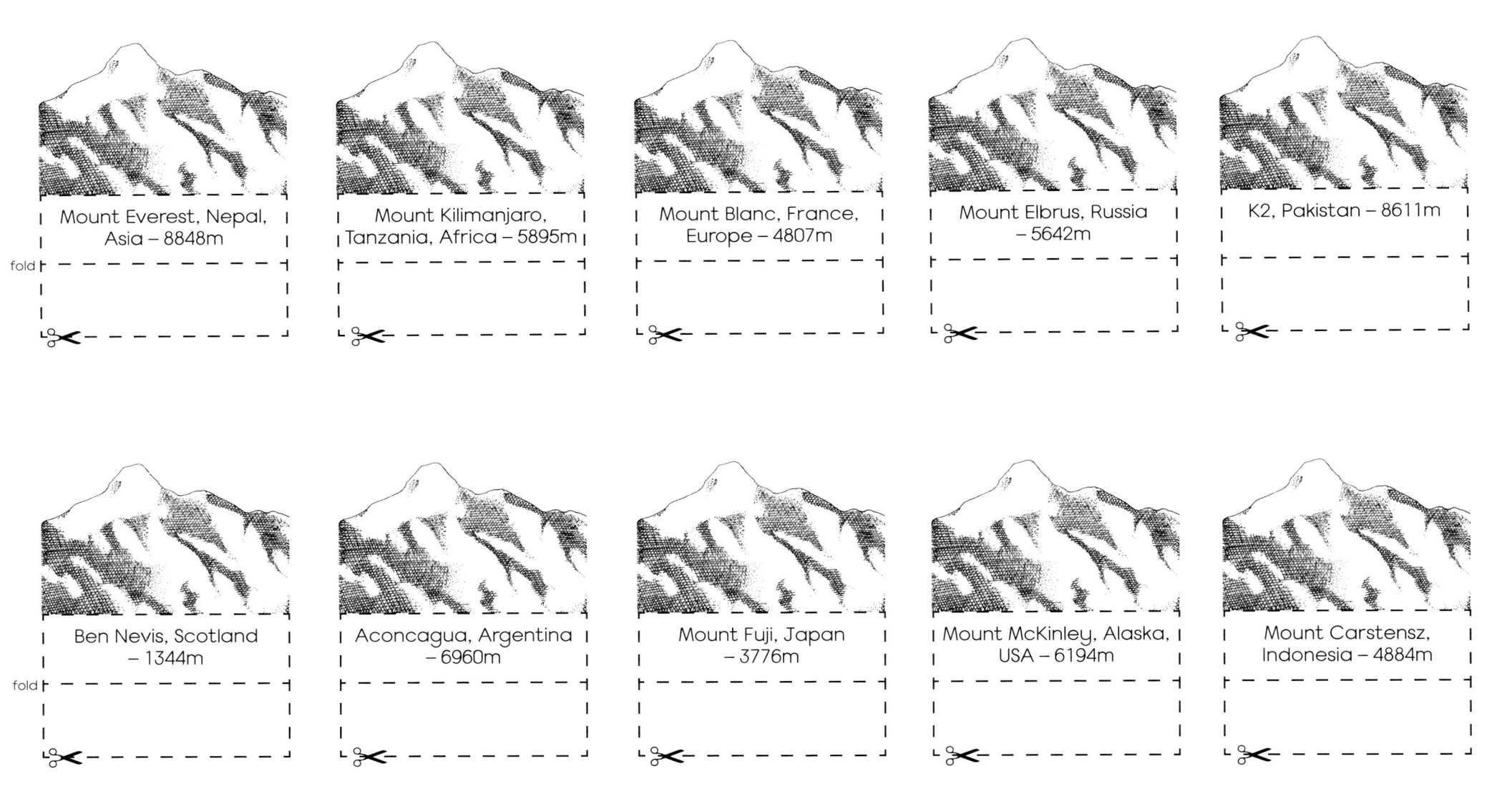

K2, Pakistan – 8611m

Mount Elbrus, Russia – 5642m

Mount Blanc, France, Europe – 4807m

Mount Kilimanjaro, Tanzania, Africa – 5895m

Mount Everest, Nepal, Asia – 8848m

Mount Carstensz, Indonesia – 4884m

Mount McKinley, Alaska, USA – 6194m

Mount Fuji, Japan – 3776m

Aconcagua, Argentina – 6960m

Ben Nevis, Scotland – 1344m

Mountain Environments

Learning Objectives

Children should:
- learn to investigate how mountain environments are similar and different in nature across a range of places and scales
- learn to use secondary sources
- learn to use ICT to access information.

Background

The landscape on mountains has been formed by the action of ice and snow over thousands of years. When snow builds up and becomes very deep, it can turn into a glacier. These tongues of ice can be several kilometres long and hundreds of metres thick. The growing pressure and weight of snow and ice, combined with the force of gravity, causes the glacier to move slowly down the valley. As it moves, pieces of broken rock accumulate underneath the ice and scour and erode the valley. Lower down the mountain, temperatures are higher and the glacier melts in the warmer air, producing a stream of melt water that flows towards the lower mountain slopes.

Glaciers produce a number of mountain features. U-shaped valleys are formed when a glacier gouges land out from narrow V-shaped valleys. Hanging valleys are created when a V-shaped valley meets a deeper glaciated valley, often leaving the stream that flowed there suspended several hundred metres above it. The streams may fall into the main valley floor below as a spectacular waterfall. Finger lakes or ribbon lakes are found where glacial melt water accumulates in long deep hollows, carved out by a glacier that has since melted and receded up the valley into the higher mountain. When a valley completely fills with ice, it may spill over its sides into a neighbouring valley and erode the land between them, cutting away a deep trench so that when they become joined together and the glacier melts, a pass is formed that people can use to move between valleys in mountain areas.

Starting Points	Main Activity	Simplified Activity	Extension Activity
M5, M6 and M7 'Artefacts (1), (2) and (3)' Discuss what an artefact is and how artefacts may help to provide evidence about a place and the lives of the people who live there. Ask the children to suggest some artefacts that they might collect to give people information about life in your area. They should give reasons for their choices. (Answers: M5 – Lake District, Grasmere; M6 – Geneva, Switzerland; M7 – Kathmandu, Nepal.)	Ask three groups of children to look carefully at the artefacts on their activity sheet. They should write what each artefact is next to the picture and look for the clues that help to locate their origin. Encourage them to discuss their findings and, together, locate the place, mountain range, country or town in an atlas from where the artefact has been collected.	Give the children copies of one of the activity sheets and ask them to identify each of the artefacts shown. Give them the names of three places that the artefacts may be from including the correct answer. Provide them with a small selection of basic atlases and some travel brochures to help them.	Ask the children to find out more about landforms in mountain areas. Give them copies of the Background, reference books and the Internet and encourage them to draw, label and make notes about the formation of mountain landforms. They should download images of different features to add to their work.

Plenary

Ask each group to talk about their activity sheet, describe each artefact and say what clues there are that provide information about the name of the mountain range, country or city the artefacts are from. Tell them to name the place and locate it on a world map or in an atlas.

Artefacts (1)

M5

- Look carefully at the collection of artefacts below. Describe each one and then try to locate the place where they have come from.

Greetings from the Lakes

FELL WALKERS REST B&B

© Folens (copiable page)   FOLENS GEOGRAPHY IN ACTION 6   11

Artefacts (2)

- Look carefully at the collection of artefacts below. Describe each one and then try to locate the place where they have come from.

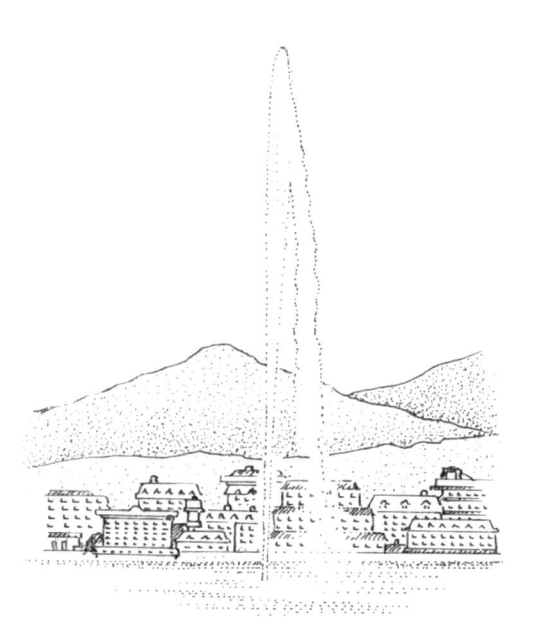

Welcome to the land of mountains, fresh air and cuckoo clocks.

Artefacts (3)

M7

- Look carefully at the collection of artefacts below. Describe each one and then try to locate the place where they have come from.

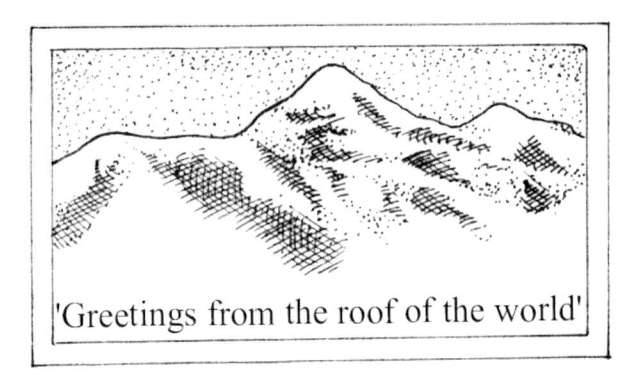

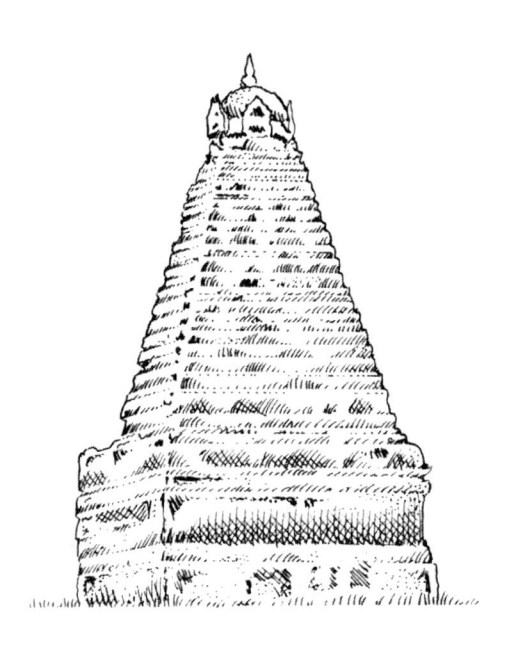

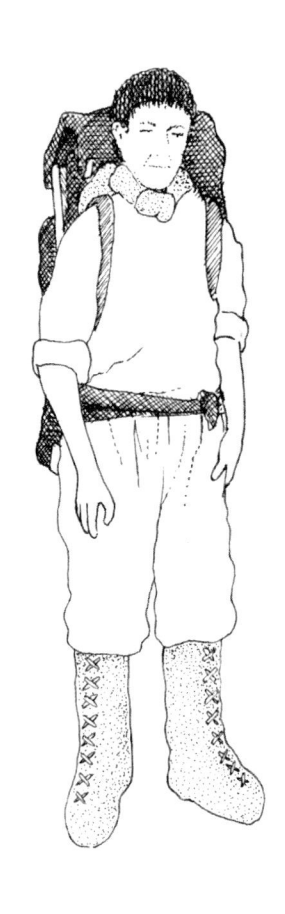

'Greetings from the roof of the world'

Yeti Tours

Come with us to the land of snow and mountains to discover the yeti

Mountains Around the World

Learning Objective

Children should:
- learn about weather patterns in different parts of the world.

Background

Mountains have a unique climate; they are generally cold, windy places but the weather can change quickly. The further up a mountain you climb, the more the temperature falls. As the air becomes thinner, there are fewer molecules and the supply of oxygen begins to fall. The capacity of the air to absorb heat from the sun is also reduced and so the temperature falls by about 5°C for every 1000m ascended. This is called the lapse rate. For example, if the temperature is 20°C at the base of a mountain, then at 4000m the temperature will have fallen to 0°C (freezing point) and at this altitude, the snowline will begin.

Winds are stronger on mountains, and blizzards can appear within minutes, causing problems for mountaineers. On high windy mountainsides, blizzards are stronger and visibility is reduced to perhaps only a few metres, putting the lives of people caught outside at risk. At times, thousands of tons of snow and ice may slide down a mountainside as an avalanche. An avalanche is caused after falls of snow, some of which may be powdery and others thick and more hard-packed, build up in layers and become unstable. Avalanches can be triggered by the weight of accumulated snow or by small changes in pressure. A skier moving across these areas can also set off an avalanche.

Starting Points	Main Activity	Simplified Activity	Extension Activity
M8 *'Climate data'* Talk about the climate of mountain areas. Explain the differences in weather and the atmospheric conditions, such as temperature, rainfall, wind speed and direction, and sunshine.	Ask the children to plot the data on simple graphs using data-handling software and compare the findings.	Help the children to plot the data for the place they previously studied. Talk to them about what the graph means and how it compares with the local climate.	Using the Internet, ask the children to find weather data for different mountain areas. Construct a graph and compare it with the graphs plotted earlier.
M9 *'White walls'* Show the children pictures of avalanches. Discuss what is happening, how the avalanche may have started and what the effects of it might be.	Look at the pictures and consider the usefulness of each avalanche defence scheme currently in use in some mountain areas. (Top picture – fences; middle picture – rockets; bottom picture – thick woodland.)	Ask the children to look at one of the avalanche defence schemes and then describe the scheme and what it is supposed to do.	Ask the children to find out more about avalanches: how they begin, move and the effects they have on human activity and people's lives.
M10 *'Mount Kilimanjaro'* Explain how weather changes with altitude, and how the weather and climate at the foot of a mountain may be completely different to that at the summit.	Talk about the vegetation and wildlife that may be found on Mount Kilimanjaro before the children complete the activity sheet.	Ask the children to describe how the temperature, vegetation and animal life will change when climbing up a mountain.	Ask the children to imagine that they are going to climb to the summit of Mount Kilimanjaro. Ask them to describe what they would pack.

Plenary

Ask the children to describe the climate and specific weather conditions that mountain areas will experience. Revise what avalanches are, how they begin and how their own scheme will reduce harm to people and damage to property.

Climate data

- Look at the climate data for each place. Draw rainfall and temperature graphs for them, either on paper or using data-handling software. Compare the graphs for each place.

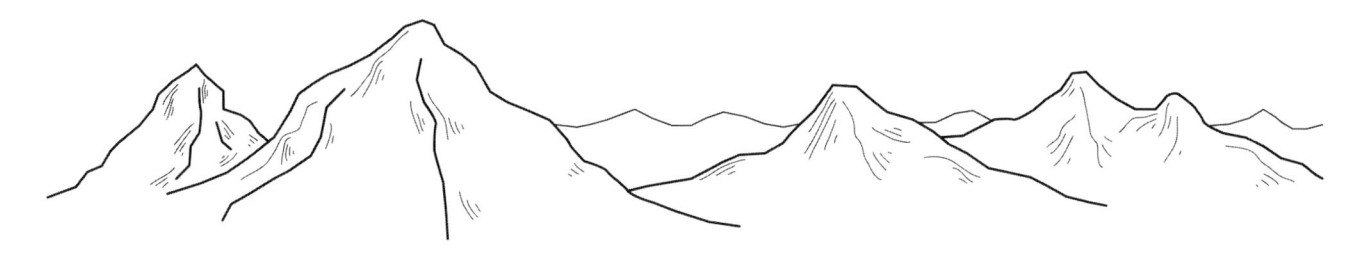

Lake District – Grasmere
Altitude 53m

Month	J	F	M	A	M	J	J	A	S	O	N	D
Temperature (°C)	6	7	9	12	16	19	20	19	17	13	9	7
Rainfall (mm)	214	146	112	101	90	111	134	139	184	196	209	215

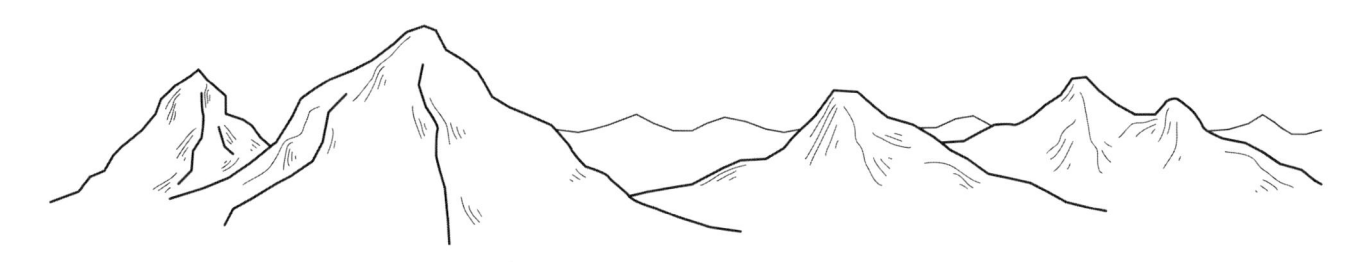

Switzerland – Geneva
Altitude 426m

Month	J	F	M	A	M	J	J	A	S	O	N	D
Temperature (°C)	1	2	6	10	14	18	19	19	16	11	6	2
Rainfall (mm)	48	46	56	64	76	79	74	91	28	41	127	125

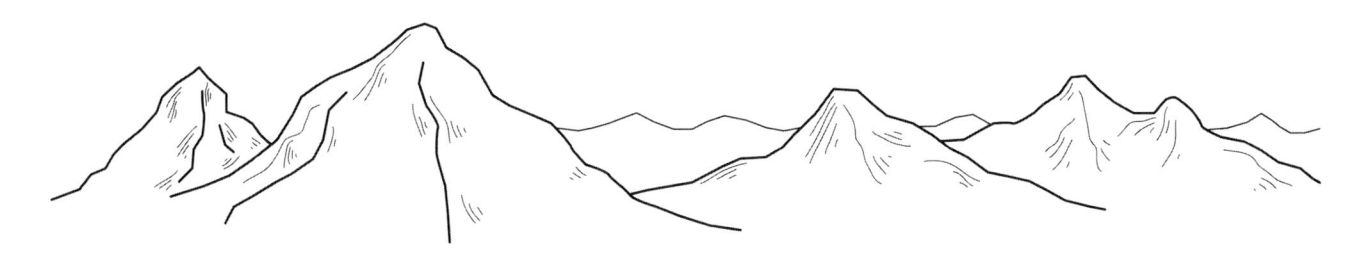

Nepal – Kathmandu
Altitude 1463m

Month	J	F	M	A	M	J	J	A	S	O	N	D
Temperature (°C)	-2	1	4	6	12	16	16	17	13	8	3	-1
Rainfall (mm)	15	41	23	58	122	246	373	345	155	28	8	3

White walls

M9

- Look at each avalanche defence scheme. Label and describe each one. Think of your own scheme, give it a title and describe how it helps to defend against avalanches.

My scheme: _____

Mount Kilimanjaro

- Use the information to draw a cross-section of Mount Kilimanjaro.

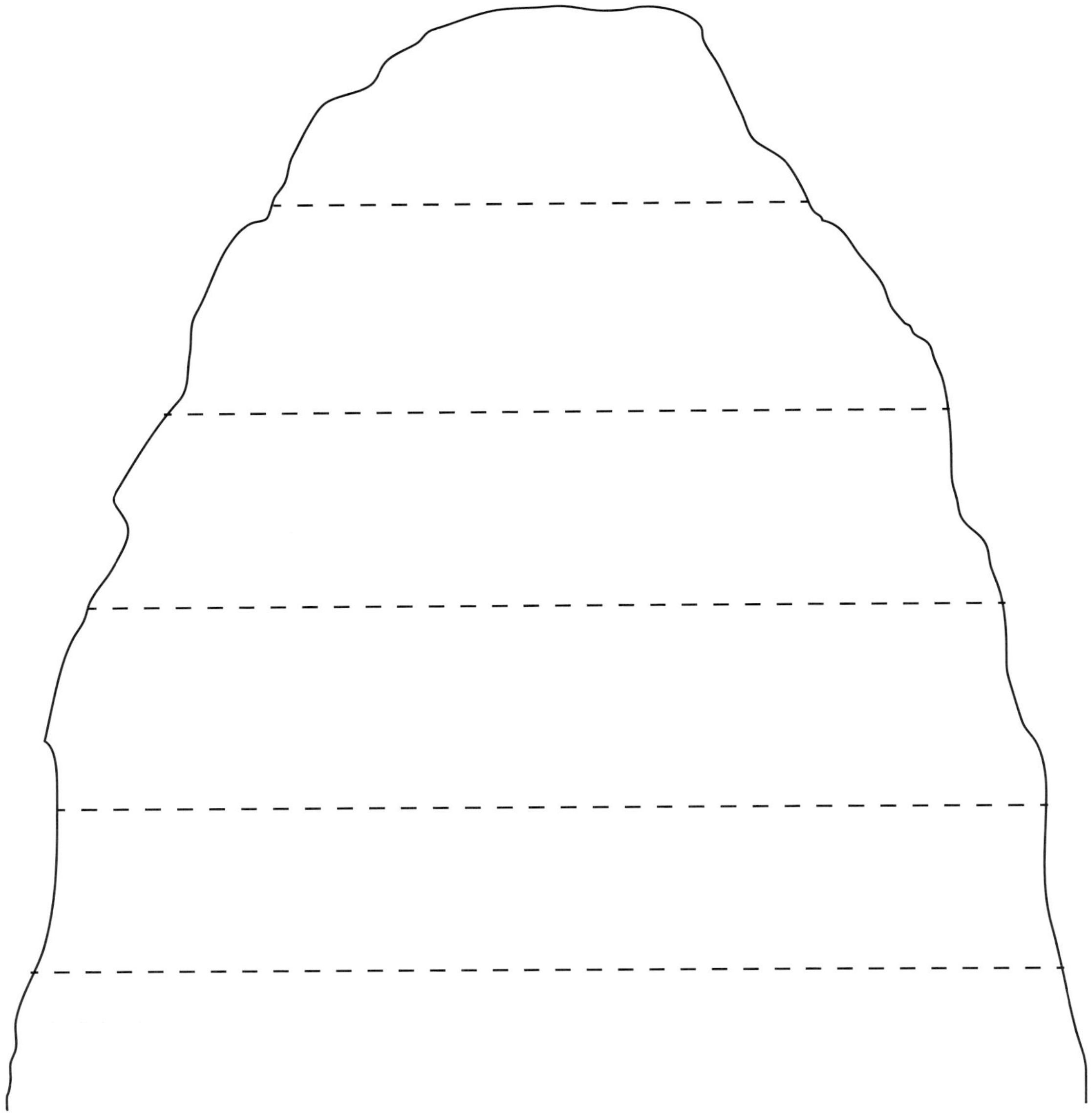

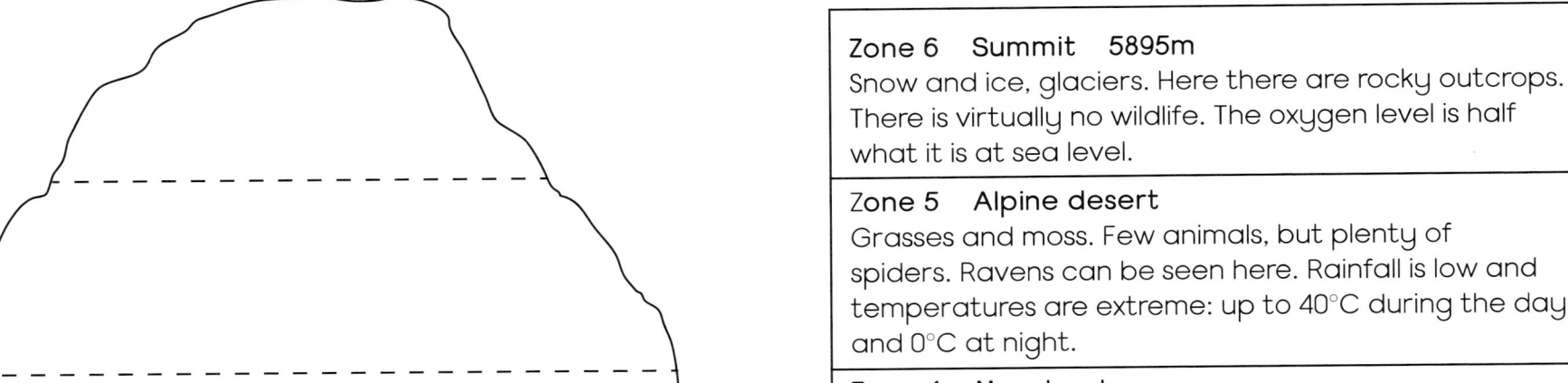

Zone 6   Summit   5895m
Snow and ice, glaciers. Here there are rocky outcrops. There is virtually no wildlife. The oxygen level is half what it is at sea level.

Zone 5   Alpine desert
Grasses and moss. Few animals, but plenty of spiders. Ravens can be seen here. Rainfall is low and temperatures are extreme: up to 40°C during the day and 0°C at night.

Zone 4   Moorland
Plants include groundsels and lobelias, which close their leaves at night to protect against frost. There are large birds of prey, elands, hunting dogs and occasional elephants.

Zone 3   Heath
Mist and fog cling to the lower edge of this zone. A cool landscape of heather, grasses, proteus, red-hot pokers and some cactus-like plants. There may be mice, rats and buzzards.

Zone 2   Rainforest
The forest receives two metres of rain a year. It is hot and humid with tall trees, palms and figs. Wildlife includes monkeys, leopards, giraffes and buffalo.

Zone 1   Cultivated areas
Crops and grasslands. Animals include hyenas and cheetahs. Chagga people live in villages in this area.

Whatever the Weather

Learning Objectives

Children should:
- learn that varying weather conditions can have a significant impact on life in an area
- learn to use secondary sources.

Background

Mountain environments can be enjoyed all the year round. In fact, many resort towns, especially in the Alps and Rocky Mountains, advertise themselves as two seasons holiday venues, with skiing holiday destinations in the winter and lakes and mountains destinations in the summer.

Although it is possible to ski in most European countries, most people from the UK travel to Alpine areas such as eastern France, Switzerland, Austria and northern Italy. In the Alps, winter snow is virtually guaranteed, especially on the higher mountain slopes, and there are usually long periods of sunshine not usually found in the northerly resorts in Norway, Sweden and Finland. Over the last few years, more distant ski resorts, such as Colorado in the USA, have become increasingly popular.

In the summer, visitors are attracted to the wooded valleys and lake and mountain scenery, which can be seen clearly in the thin, fresh mountain air. Coach tours are also very popular, with itineraries organised to allow holidaymakers to see as much of the lakes and mountain landscape as possible.

Starting Points	Main Activity	Simplified Activity	Extension Activity
M11 *'All seasons holidays'* Show the children two holiday brochures that show the same resort as both a winter and a summer destination.	Look together and talk about the empty brochure page shown on the activity sheet. Discuss with the children the kind of information, pictures and data they might include.	Fill in the blank sections on the brochure page but miss out some key words and phrases. Ask the children to add a word or phrase to give more detail about the activities.	Give the children two or three pages from a winter or summer brochure and ask them to highlight the activities in red and the weather information in blue.
M12 *'Black run'* Talk about skiing on Alpine slopes. Discuss what the different coloured runs are like and how they demand different skills from the skier (black – very difficult, yellow – quite easy).	Follow the instructions on the activity sheet to play the game.	Ask the children to draw onto the activity sheet the route the skier may take to get to the finish line. Ask them to calculate the distance using string and measure it against a ruler.	Ask the children to draw their own black run on a separate piece of paper, asking them to include various hazards that a skier may encounter.
M13 *'Lakes and mountains'* Together, look at the itineraries of some of the coach tours around Alpine areas in the summer, usually found in lakes and mountains holiday brochures.	Discuss the task with the children before they complete the activity sheet.	Talk to the children about the map and ask them to describe one or two journeys to one or two features from different hotels.	Ask the children to write down their tour itinerary as it would be shown in a travel brochure. Ask them to follow another itinerary using a map and work out the distance the coach travels each day. Write the total distance travelled on the itinerary.

Plenary

Cut out pictures of people enjoying summer and winter activities in the mountains. Make two collages under the titles 'Mountains in the summer' and 'Mountains in the winter'. Ask the children to discuss what kind of mountain holiday they would prefer and why.

All seasons holidays

M11

- Make this page into a summer 'Lakes and Mountains' brochure page or a 'Winter Skiing' brochure page.

Location of the hotel

Hotel facilities

Resort activities

Weather information

Activities further away

Prices

Black run

M12

- For each turn, choose the direction you wish to ski in. Roll the die to see how far you can travel. The amount on the die is equal to the amount of centimetres that you can travel, for example, if you roll a four, you can travel up to four centimetres in your chosen direction. Measure, with a ruler, the distance you are going to travel and mark it in, gradually drawing your route down the mountain. If you overestimate the distance to travel or choose the wrong direction, you will go outside of the run, hitting trees or rocks, and you may even collide with your opponent. In each of these cases, you must miss a turn. You can set off again on the run nearest to the place at which you crashed. The first to the bottom wins.

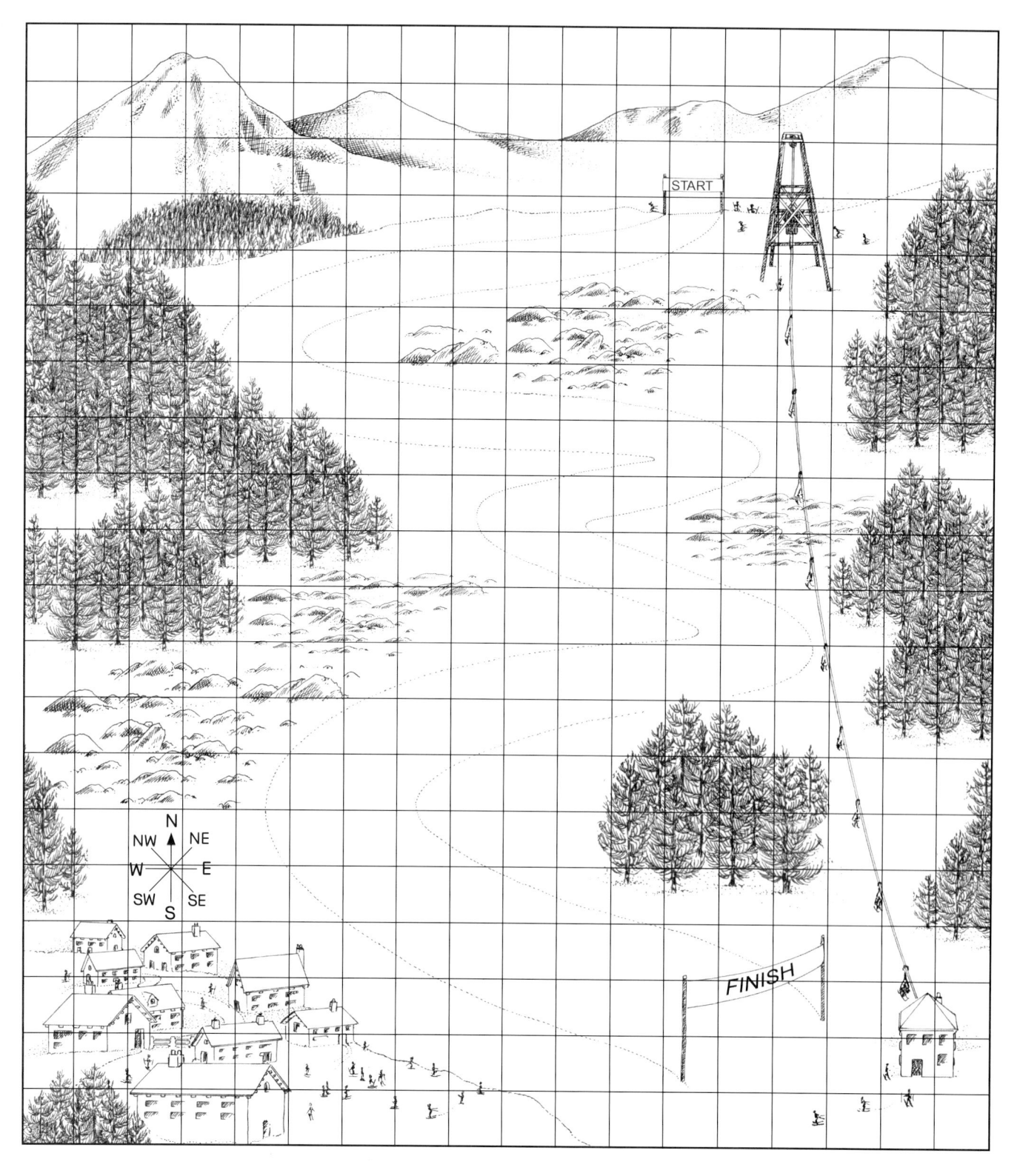

Lakes and mountains

M13

- Make a coach tour itinerary for one week that visits as many different towns and sights as possible. Travel up to 100km each day. Stay at a different hotel each night. Include two or three rest days and return to the hotel you started from.

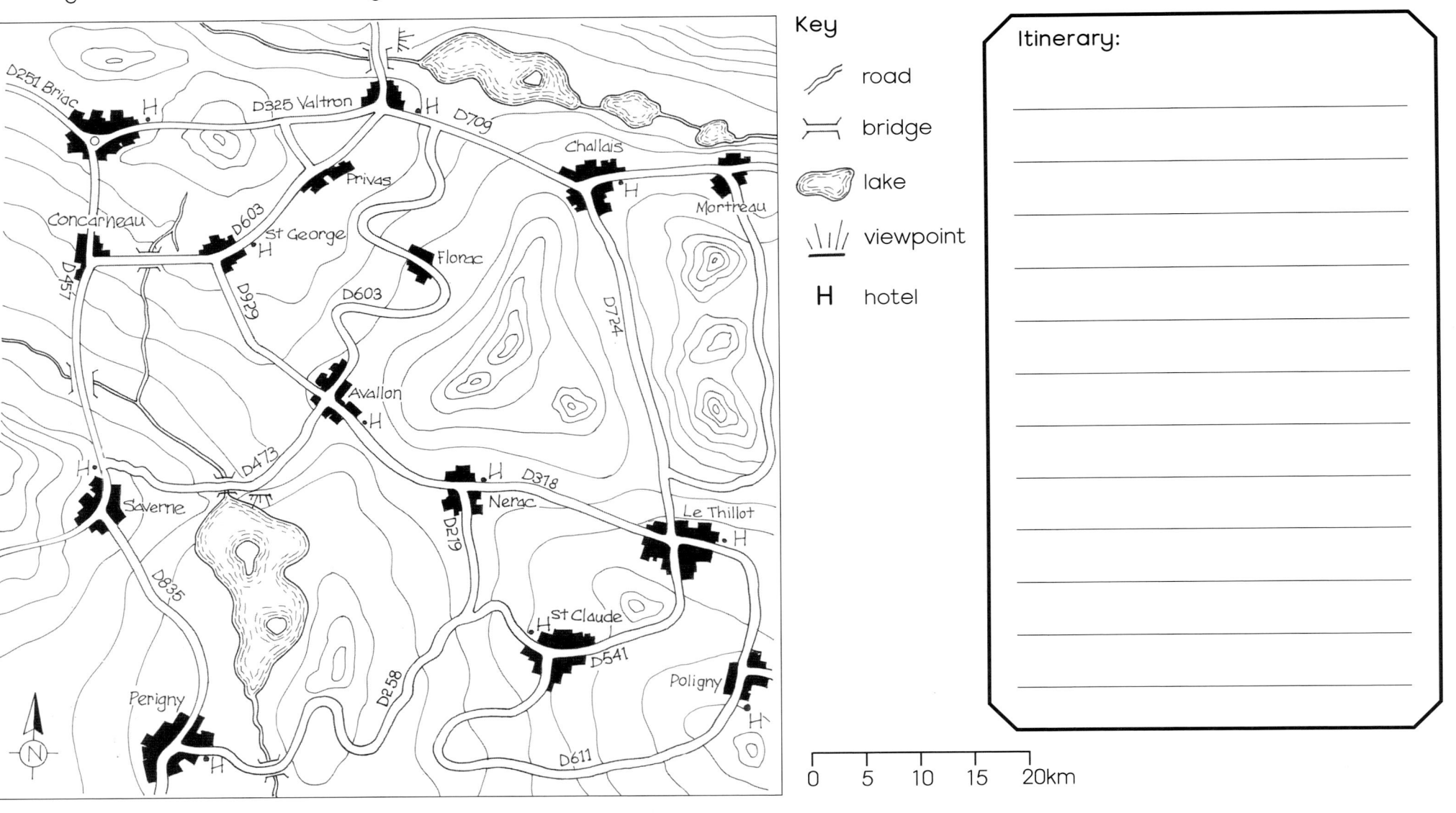

Itinerary:

Key
- road
- bridge
- lake
- viewpoint
- H hotel

Scale: 0 5 10 15 20km

The Highest Junkyard in the World

Learning Objective

Children should:
- learn that the effect of tourism can be significant in a given area and can be both good and bad.

Background

Mountain areas represent almost 20% of the global tourist industry. The Alps alone count for about 10% of mountain tourism, with the Rocky Mountains and Himalayas not far behind. The seasonal influx of tourists has a great effect on the character of towns and villages. Tourism is not evenly spread throughout mountain areas and so the effect that tourists have on local resources and on the fragile mountain environment is also uneven. Tourists are a mixed blessing as they bring money into areas that may normally be poor farming communities. Local people are employed in hotels, restaurants and shops or as guides and instructors. It is a strange irony that tourists damage the environment that they come to enjoy. One of the biggest problems is litter. The Mount Everest region has been named 'the world's highest junkyard', and the trail to the Everest base camp, 'the garbage trail', as there is an estimated 17 tons of rubbish per kilometre along it.

Starting Points	Main Activity	Simplified Activity	Extension Activity
M14 *'The world's highest junkyard'* Discuss how tourism might affect the settlements and landscape the tourists have come to visit.	Look at the pictures and ask the children to describe the problem and a solution for each one.	Bring in a hiking boot, empty drinks cans and a toy car. On sticky notes, ask the children to write how the people who use each one are damaging mountain areas. Attach the sticky note to each item.	Ask the children to undertake some research to find out about other problems facing mountain environments.
M15 *'Mixed blessing'* Discuss how tourists can be a mixed blessing to the local people and their environment.	Ask the children to sort out the advantages and disadvantages of tourists coming to mountain areas.	Write a mixed-up list of good and bad things about tourism in mountain areas. Ask the children to cut them out and put them into groups labelled 'Tourism – good' and 'Tourism – bad'.	Ask the children to write an article for a local Swiss newspaper describing the effects of tourism on mountain communities.
M16 *'Quiet village – crowded resort'* Ask the children to imagine that they live in a Swiss village. Discuss the changes seen as the village developed into a resort over the years.	Ask the children to describe the village in the first box and how it has changed in the second box.	Ask the children to look at the bottom picture and describe how the town caters for winter tourists.	Encourage the children to draw and label a map of the village shown in the first picture and the town shown in the second picture. They should note the changes that have occurred.
M17 *'Sign of the times'* Look at some of the different advertisements found in magazines and ask the children to think about a poster advertisement to encourage people to look after the mountains.	Ask the children to design a poster to encourage tourists to look after the mountains.	Provide a caption which gives a strong indication to the problem. Discuss what the problem is, how the slogan is trying to highlight it and then ask the children to design the image.	Ask the children to look at the posters designed by other children, select the best one and explain why this poster would encourage tourists to look after the mountains.

Plenary

Ask pairs of children to talk about the language they used and the images they decided to show on their posters. Make a display of them.

The world's highest junkyard

M14

- Below are some drawings of problems created by tourists. Label what each problem is and what a solution to the problem might be.

Problem: _____

Solution: _____

Problem: _____

Solution: _____

Problem: _____

Solution: _____

Problem: _____

Solution: _____

© Folens (copiable page)   FOLENS GEOGRAPHY IN ACTION 6   23

Mixed blessing

M15

- Sort out the good and bad effects of tourism in mountain areas by highlighting the good effects in green and the bad effects in red. Write a few sentences to explain some of the statements.

crowds

animals eat food left by tourists

jobs for local people

noise from people/cars

litter

young people stay instead of moving away to find work

extra local income

lots of building work

higher standard of living for local people

alpine areas opened up for people to enjoy

new roads have made small communities more accessible

over-developed villages

traffic congestion

footpath erosion

extra demand on resources

removing trees to make room for ski runs can cause avalanches

Quiet village – crowded resort

- Look at how this Alpine village has changed over the last 30 years. Describe the village in the first box and how it has changed in the second box.

Sign of the times

- Design a poster to encourage tourists to look after the mountains.

Holidays in the Mountains

Learning Objective

Children should:
- learn how the environment affects the nature of human activity.

Background

Millions of people head for the hills each year to explore mountain areas and enjoy the scenery and fresh air. In mountain areas the weather can change rapidly. It is important to take proper clothing that is windproof, waterproof and warm, even if the forecast predicts fine weather.

Care needs to be taken when pitching a tent, for example, away from rivers and streams in case there is a flash flood. These are caused by torrential rain running over hard ground rather than soaking into it, heading directly into streams and rivers. During flash floods, rivers quickly burst their banks and strong currents can wash away tents or trap campers in quickly rising waters.

Starting Points	Main Activity	Simplified Activity	Extension Activity
M18 *'Under canvas'* Talk about camping: where children have been, how they prepared for it and the activities they undertook.	Tell the children that the letters on the picture show possible camping sites. Ask them to describe the advantages and disadvantages of each one and to select the best place (site D).	Reduce the number of possible sites to two or three, (leaving in site D as this is in the best location). Encourage the children to talk about the sites and to give a reason for their final choice.	Ask groups of children to try to erect a tent in the school grounds after first selecting a good site. Ask them to say why they chose the site.
M19 *'Head for the hills'* Ask the children to describe the equipment and clothes they would take with them for a day's trek into the mountains.	The activity sheet shows various items that a camper could take on a long mountain walk. Ask the children to cut out and rank ten of the items, starting with the most important.	Reduce the number of items the camper should take to five and follow the task described in the Main Activity.	Together, look at each of the items and say how each may be of use to the camper on a long walk (some are of little use). Encourage a debate and then agree on ten items to take.
M20 and **M21** *'Mountain trek (1) and (2)'* Allow the children a few minutes to look at a 1:50 000 OS map of your local area. Direct their attention to the way that contour lines are drawn.	Looking at M20, ask the children to describe the landscape shown by contour lines on the map. Looking at the 'photographs' on M21, which were taken along the route on M20, they should work out the exact location of each 'photograph', giving a four-figure grid reference, and the direction the camera lens was pointing in.	Encourage the children to look carefully at each 'photograph' on M21 and ask them to describe what they can see. Help the children to give four-figure grid references for some physical and human features on M20.	Ask the children to describe the walk on M20 from the campsite at the Lodge, around the mountains and valleys, following the footpath shown. Ask them to write an A4 folded leaflet about the walk.

Plenary

Ask individual children to describe the equipment and clothes they would take with them on the walk in the mountains shown on M20.

Under canvas

- In pairs, discuss the best site for a family to pitch their tent. On a separate piece of paper, write five short paragraphs describing the advantages and disadvantages of each pitch. Which one is best?

M18

Head for the hills

- Imagine that you are going on a day's walk high into the mountains. Cut out and then rank ten items in order of importance that you would wear or take with you. Give a reason as to why you have chosen each one.

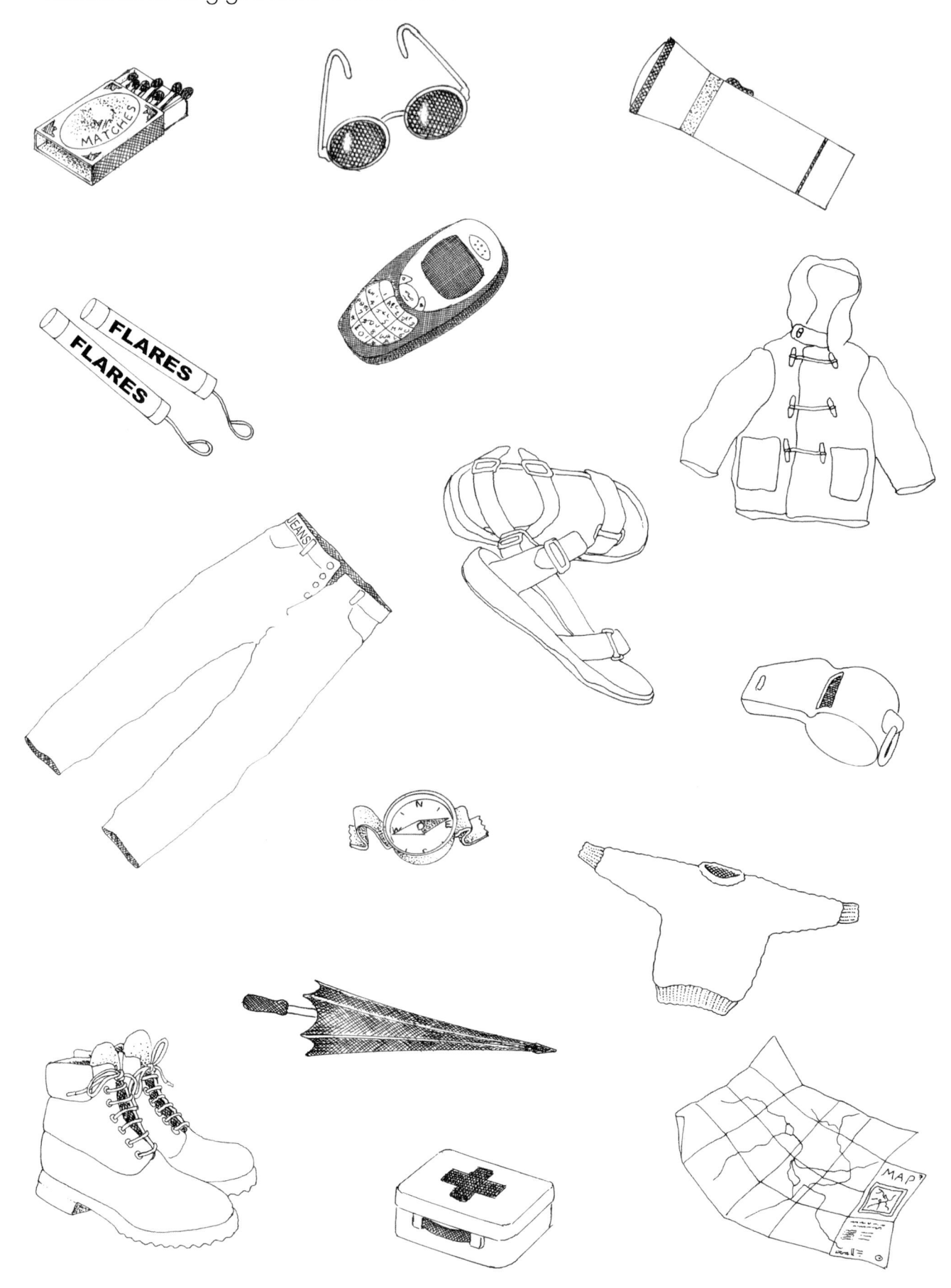

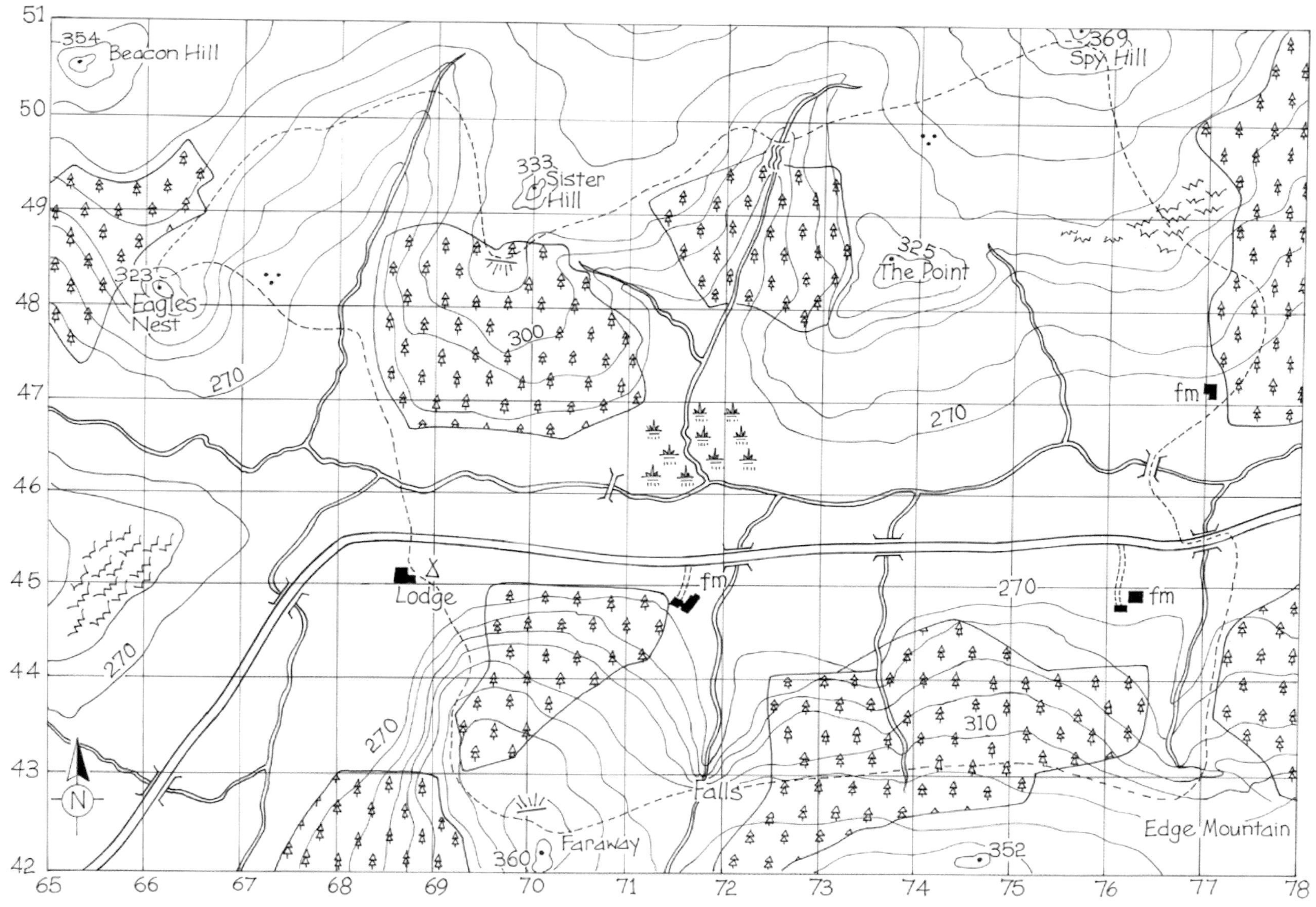

Mountain trek (1)

Key
- viewpoint
- bridge
- crags
- farm (fm)
- marsh
- woodland
- footpath
- springs
- rapids

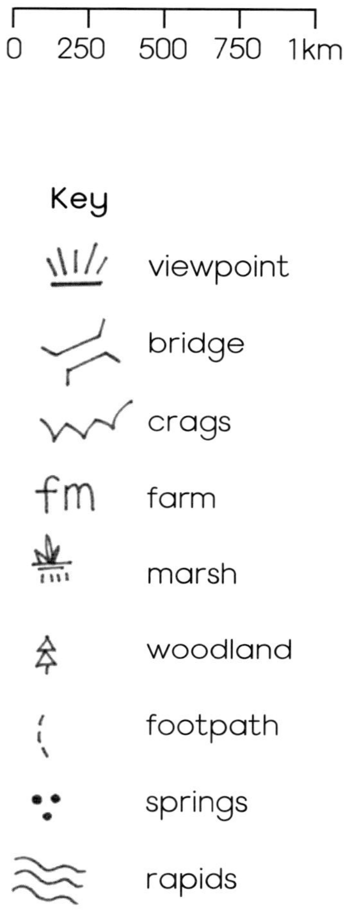

Scale: 0, 250, 500, 750, 1km

Mountain trek (2)

M21

- Look at the map on M20 and the 'photographs' below. On the map, mark where you think each 'photograph' was taken with the number of the 'photograph' and a small arrow to show the direction of the view. Write the grid reference of each location in the boxes above each picture below.

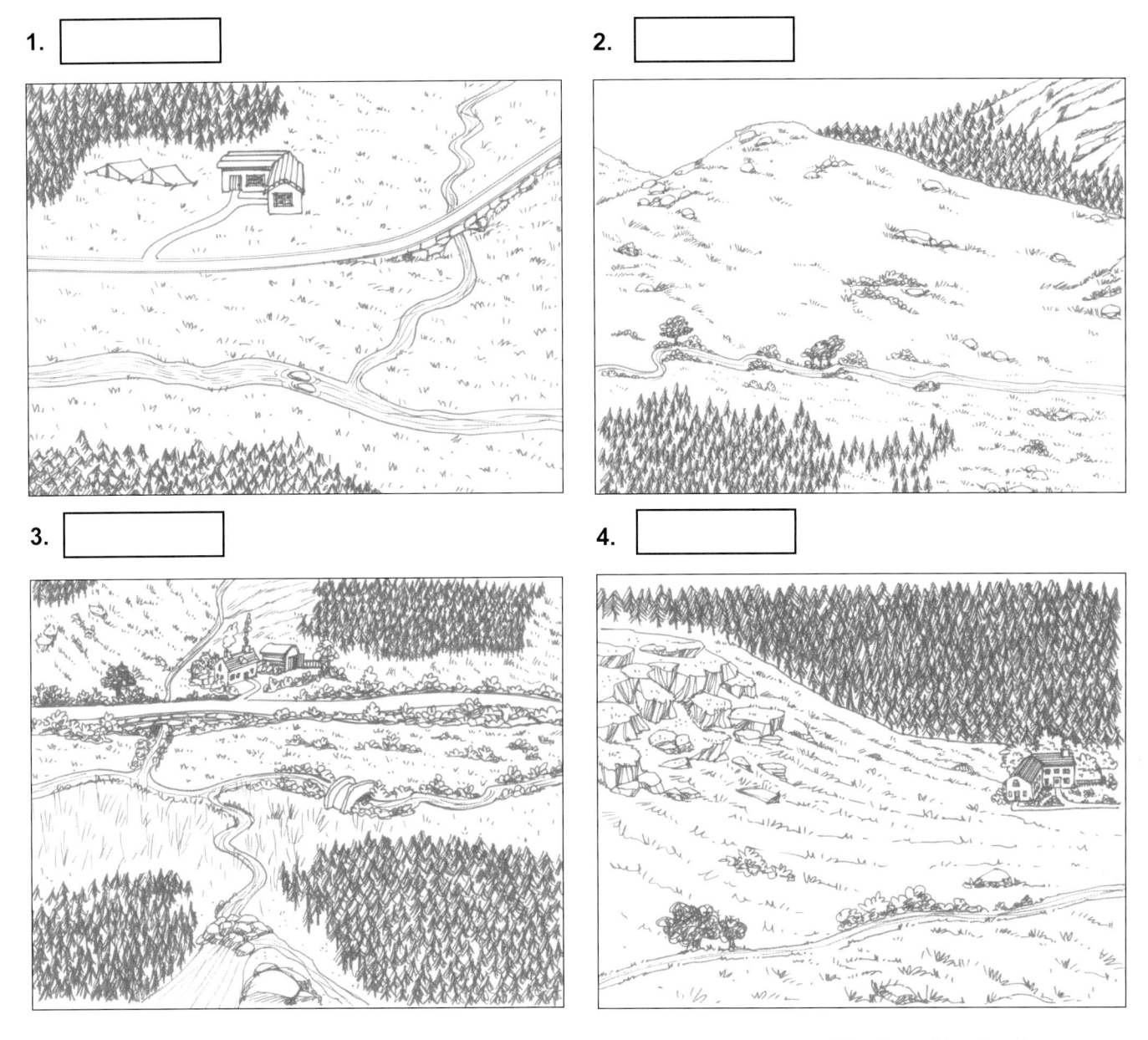

1. ☐

2. ☐

3. ☐

4. ☐

- On a separate piece of paper, describe a walk from the Lodge. Mention the features that you pass or come close to on the walk.
- Give a grid reference for a place that has a:

   steep slope ☐

   medium slope ☐

   gentle slope ☐

   What do the contour lines look like at these places?

© Folens (copiable page)   FOLENS GEOGRAPHY IN ACTION 6   31

Changing Coastlines

Learning Objectives

Children should:
- use maps and atlases to locate coasts
- understand that the sea erodes and deposits material to form a variety of features.

Background

The coast is unique as it is the place where the three elements meet (water, land and air). It is through the action of moving air, or wind on the surface of the sea, that waves are made. These waves batter the coastline, producing a variety of landscape features. Coastal environments change at a rate determined by the hardness of the rocks and the strength and frequency of the waves that crash against them. As a result, some areas of coastline are being eroded more quickly than others and where the waves and currents are weaker, material is being laid down instead, building up other areas of the coastline.

Starting Points	Main Activity	Simplified Activity	Extension Activity
C1 *'Coast to coast'* Look at and discuss a variety of typical postcard scenes. Find out where the children have been to on holiday in the UK and locate these on a wall map.	Ask the children to describe each postcard and find out and name the different resort. Locate with a dot your local area and, on the map, ask the children to work out, using the compass and scale, the direction and straight line distance to each seaside resort.	Supply the children with an amended activity sheet on which each of the seaside towns are named. Include an eight-point compass; straight lines should also be drawn from your town to each resort. Ask the children to work out the direction and straight-line distance to each resort.	Cut out named pictures of foreign coastal resorts. Ask the children to locate each one in an atlas and note the direction and distance to them from your town.
C2 *'Breakers'* Introduce the idea that coastlines are constantly changing and that some parts are being worn away to form distinctive coastal landforms.	This activity sheet will be a glossary page. Using reference books, ask the children to find out about each feature and add a short description from the teacher.	Write a short description of each feature on sticky notes. Ask the children to read each one out and stick them next to the correct picture.	Using the Internet, ask the children to download images of features caused by coastal erosion and locate them on wall maps. They should name each one and attach them to the appropriate map.
C3 *'Deposition'* Explain how waves break material from the coast and how currents transport this material down the coast so it is laid down or deposited in a series of unique landforms.	Discuss each of the descriptions. Using reference books and the Internet, ask the children to draw in the appropriate picture and to label each one.	Draw a quick sketch of each feature on a sticky note. Together, read each description again and ask the children to attach the sticky note to the correct box.	Ask the children to write about the process of deposition that resulted in each feature being formed.

Plenary

Ask some of the children to read out some of their descriptions, as if they are the teacher. See if others can explain how features of erosion are formed.

Coast to coast

C1

- Each postcard place is marked on the map of the British Isles with a dot. Use an atlas and look at each postcard to work out where each one was sent from. Locate your area on the map and mark it with a dot. Work out the direction and straight-line distance from your area to each postcard place using the compass and scale.

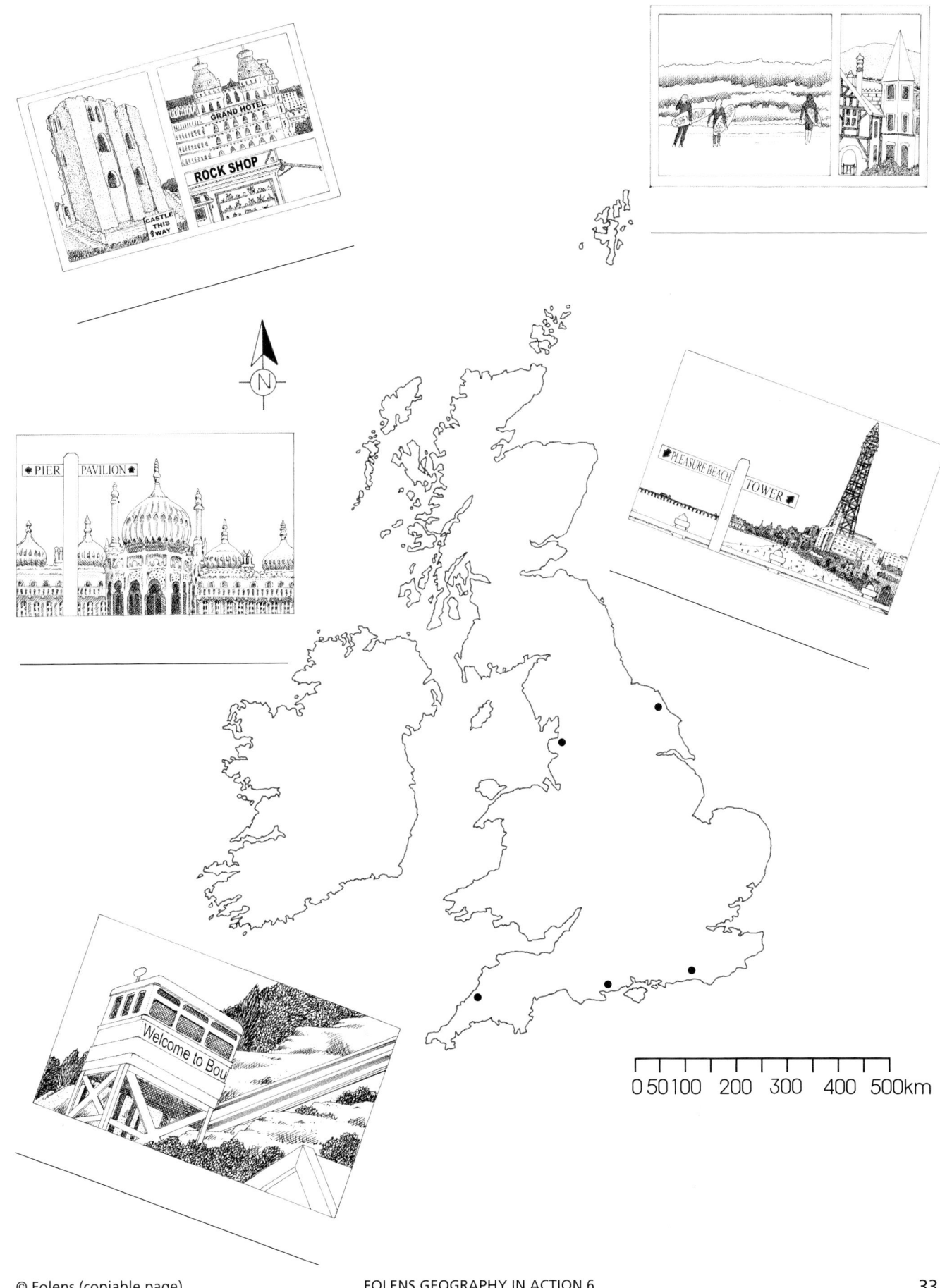

0 50 100 200 300 400 500km

© Folens (copiable page)   FOLENS GEOGRAPHY IN ACTION 6

Breakers

C2

- In the teacher's speech bubbles, write a description of how each coastal feature is formed by erosion.

Cliff

Sea arch

Sea stack

Sea cave

Wave-cut platform

Deposition

- Use the descriptions to help you to work out the four different depositional features. Sketch and label each one.

A strip of fine material deposited by the sea by the action of the waves and longshore drift. These are usually wide and gently shelving.

A ridge of sand running away from the coast, usually with a curved end. These grow in the direction of longshore drift.

A narrow, steep strip of rounded pebbles. These have been deposited by the action of the waves and longshore drift.

A low ridge of sand slightly out to sea and usually parallel to the shore. They are often visible at low tide and often occur between headlands.

Coastal Erosion

Learning Objectives

Children should:
- learn to communicate to others using appropriate geographical vocabulary
- learn to use secondary sources including maps and atlases
- learn about the physical features of coasts and how they are formed.

Background

Cliffs are steep, rocky walls that are being constantly attacked by destructive waves. Cliffs form most effectively in resistant rocks that wear away more slowly than those made of softer rocks, which crumble under attack from powerful waves. As cliffs are slowly eroded, they retreat leaving a flat surface called a wave-cut platform or abrasion ramp, stretching from the base of the cliff to the sea.

Most erosion occurs at the foot of the cliff where the pressure of the waves is greater and the rock is under constant bombardment by the pebbles and rocks that the waves contain. This process is known as undercutting. As this part of the cliff erodes, the weight of material above causes the area of the cliff closest to the sea to collapse, fall into the sea and be washed away. Areas of resistant rock that jut out into the sea are known as headlands. Within the cliff face there will be areas of softer rock or areas where the rock is weak or faulted. Here erosion is more rapid. The sea wears away the weaker rock or widens the faults through the headland to form a rock arch. This will slowly increase in size until the top of the arch collapses into the sea, leaving behind a stack, a column of rock separated from the receding headland by the sea.

Starting Points	Main Activity	Simplified Activity	Extension Activity
C4 *'Mapping the coast'* Talk about coastal erosion and the process involved in creating the landforms associated with it.	Together, identify the features of erosion and deposition shown. Ask the children to draw and label a map of this section of coastline.	Draw a simple map of a coastal area. Ask the children to label it using a word bank.	Look at a 1:25 000 OS map of a coastal area. Ask the children to locate and give six-figure grid references for landforms created by erosion and deposition.
C5 *'Cliff attack'* Make a sandcastle. Talk about cliffs and how they are undercut by waves. Gradually remove sand out from the base of the sandcastle to represent wave action and talk about the process that occurs.	Explain the process of erosion once again. Ask the children to label the diagrams and then write a short paragraph describing the process.	Rebuild the sandcastle. Discuss cliff erosion through undercutting again. Put some small plastic or wooden bricks on the cliff edge and ask the children to say what will happen to the buildings built there.	Using the Internet, ask the children to find out more about particular coastal landmarks, such as the Old Man of Hoy, the Needles and the White Cliffs of Dover. Ask them to download images, label them and describe how each was formed.
C6 *'Holbeck Hall Hotel'* Together, use the Internet to find out about Holbeck Hall Hotel in Scarborough which collapsed into the sea in 1993. Talk about the reasons why the hotel collapsed.	Ask the children to cut out the statements and arrange them in the correct order to tell the story of Holbeck Hall Hotel.	Cut out the statements and give the children a smaller amount to put in order. Ask them to describe the collapse of the hotel and write a short paragraph about it.	Ask the children to find out more about landslides, how they occur and the effects they can have on the landscape and people's lives.

Plenary

Ask some of the children to describe the process of cliff collapse and refer to enlargements of the diagrams shown on C5. Ask one of the children to describe the process using a sandcastle. Together, rearrange the statements from C6 and describe the collapse of Holbeck Hall Hotel.

Mapping the coast

- Draw and label a map of the section of coastline shown below. Identify the features of erosion and deposition that you can find.

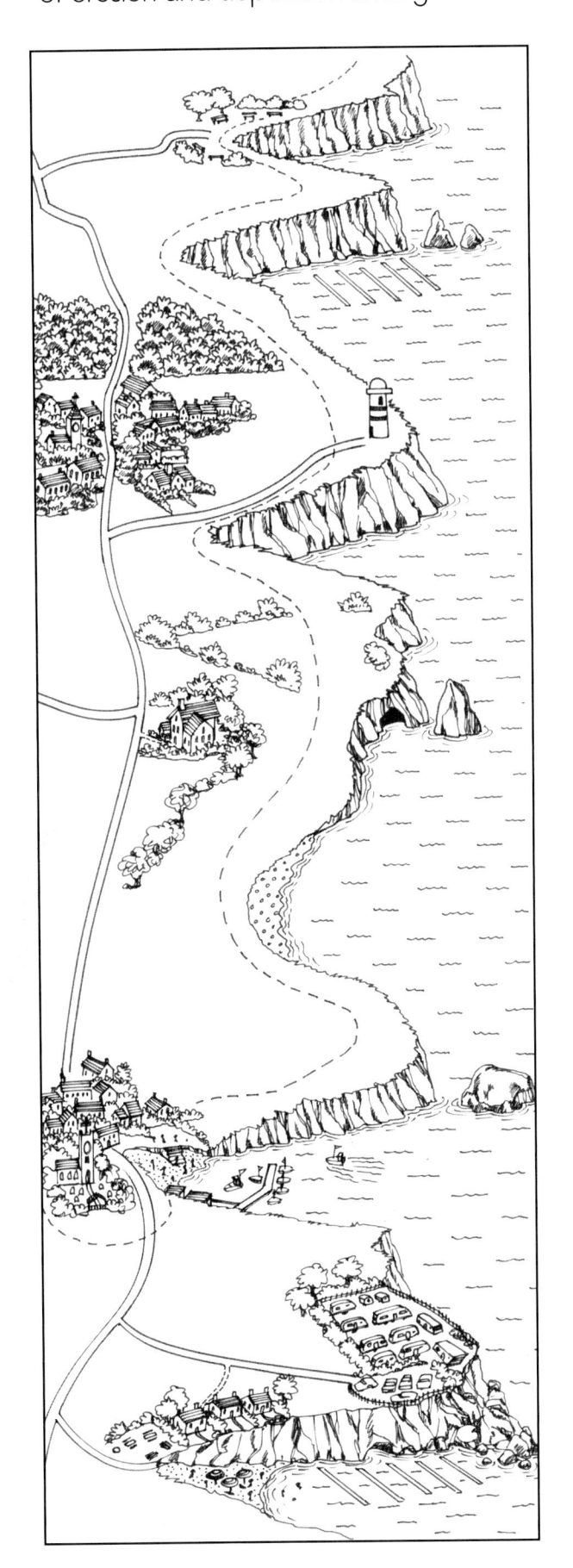

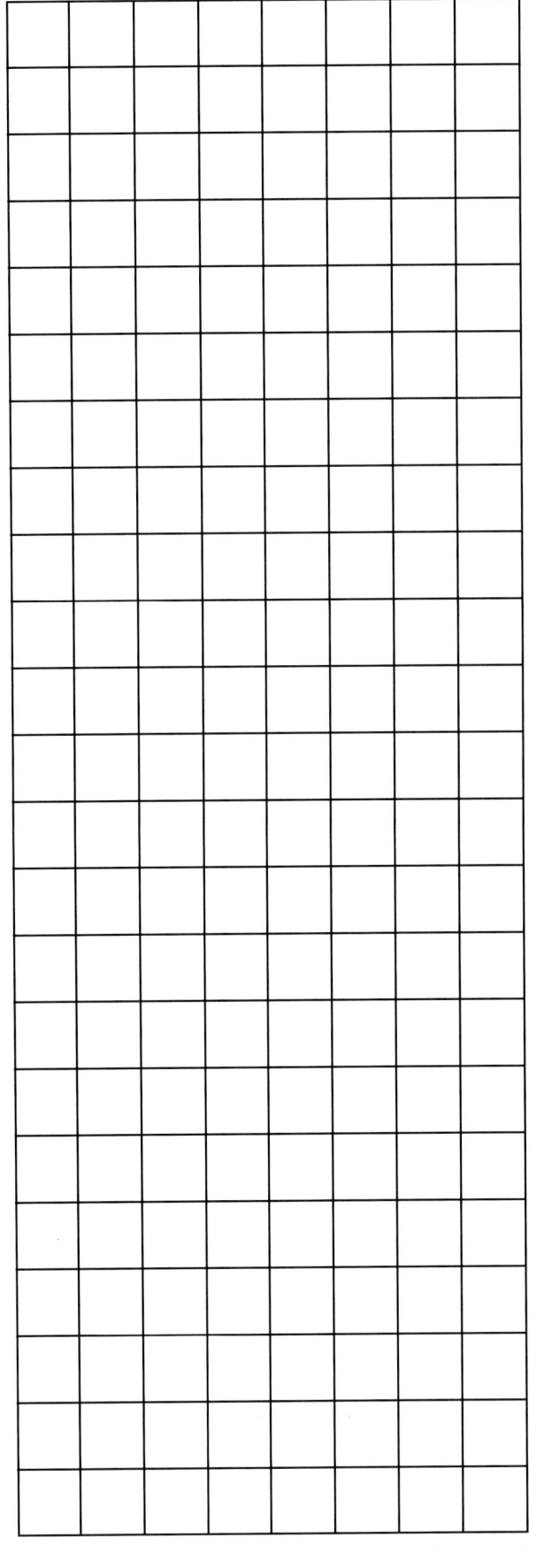

Cliff attack

- Label the diagrams that show how cliffs are eroded. Write short paragraphs to describe the processes.

Holbeck Hall Hotel

- Cut out and put the statements in order to tell the story of Holbeck Hall Hotel.

Good drains may have prevented a landslip.

The remains of the hotel were unsafe and demolished at a cost of £500 000.

The cliff it stood on was composed of unstable bands of different rock and clay, which can slip.

Stabilising trees were removed to give a good view of the North Sea.

The original house was built in 1887.

The hotel collapsed one day in June 1993.

Everyone was evacuated and no one was hurt.

There had been a lot of rain before the collapse.

There were small landslips in 1982 and 1986.

Holbeck Hall was a four-star hotel set 65m above the sea at South Cliff in Scarborough.

Beaches

Learning Objectives

Children should:
- learn to use appropriate geographical vocabulary, maps and secondary sources of information
- learn the location of places and environments they study
- learn about the physical features of coasts and the processes of deposition that affect them.

Background

Many coastlines show features of deposition. Waves transport material that has been eroded along the coast in a process known as longshore drift and when this material is deposited, new landforms, such as beaches, are built-up. Waves carrying sand and gravel pushed by the wind, break at an angle to the beach, and some of the material they carry is laid down. When the coastline changes direction, for example, at a headland, the material carried by the waves is laid down in a finger-shaped deposit called a spit. When headlands are joined together by deposits of sand and shingle, a bar is created. These can, over time, block the entrances to ports and harbours unless the area where material is deposited is frequently dredged.

Beaches may be composed of sand or shingle. Some coasts may contain rounded accumulations of sand in the form of dunes. These are very unstable but over time can become covered in marram grass, which helps to stabilise the dunes.

Starting Points	Main Activity	Simplified Activity	Extension Activity
C7 'On the beach' Together, look at a 1:25 000 or 1:50 000 OS map and use the key to identify sand and shingle beaches.	Ask the children to locate each beach and activity shown using six-figure grid references. They should colour the map.	Ask the children to use four-figure grid references to locate different beaches and activities.	Look at some of the different areas of coastline in the UK. Ask the children to write about the different features and note how the areas differ.
C8 'Longshore drift' Explain the process of longshore drift and how it is responsible for coastal erosion.	Ask the children to describe the process of longshore drift.	Write down statements that describe the process of longshore drift and ask the children, in pairs, to put them in the correct order.	Ask the children to find out more about parts of the coast which have high levels of erosion.
C9 'Dune' Talk about the formation of sand dunes and how blown sand will collect around objects such as rocks and stones.	Ask the children to write about a walk from X to Y and talk about the landscape, land use and plant life.	Ask the children to add captions to the picture saying what the land is being used for and what the landscape is like.	Fill a large shallow tray with dry sharp sand. On it, place pebbles of varying sizes, some close together and others further apart. From one end of the tray, fan the sand and, together, look at a dune landscape beginning to form.
C10 'Spurn Head' Describe how longshore drift is responsible for the creation of spits.	Together, find Spurn Head in an atlas. Ask the children to label the field sketch of Spurn Head using information gained from the Internet or the word bank. They should draw a small locational map of the sketch.	Encourage the children to use the word bank to label the sketch and to find images of Spurn Head on the Internet.	Scan and copy the activity sheet to display on the interactive whiteboard. Encourage the children to describe its formation and label features on and around it.

Plenary

Talk about longshore drift and the effect it has on our coastal landscape and scenery.

On the beach

C7

- Give a six-figure grid reference for each beach and activity shown on the map.

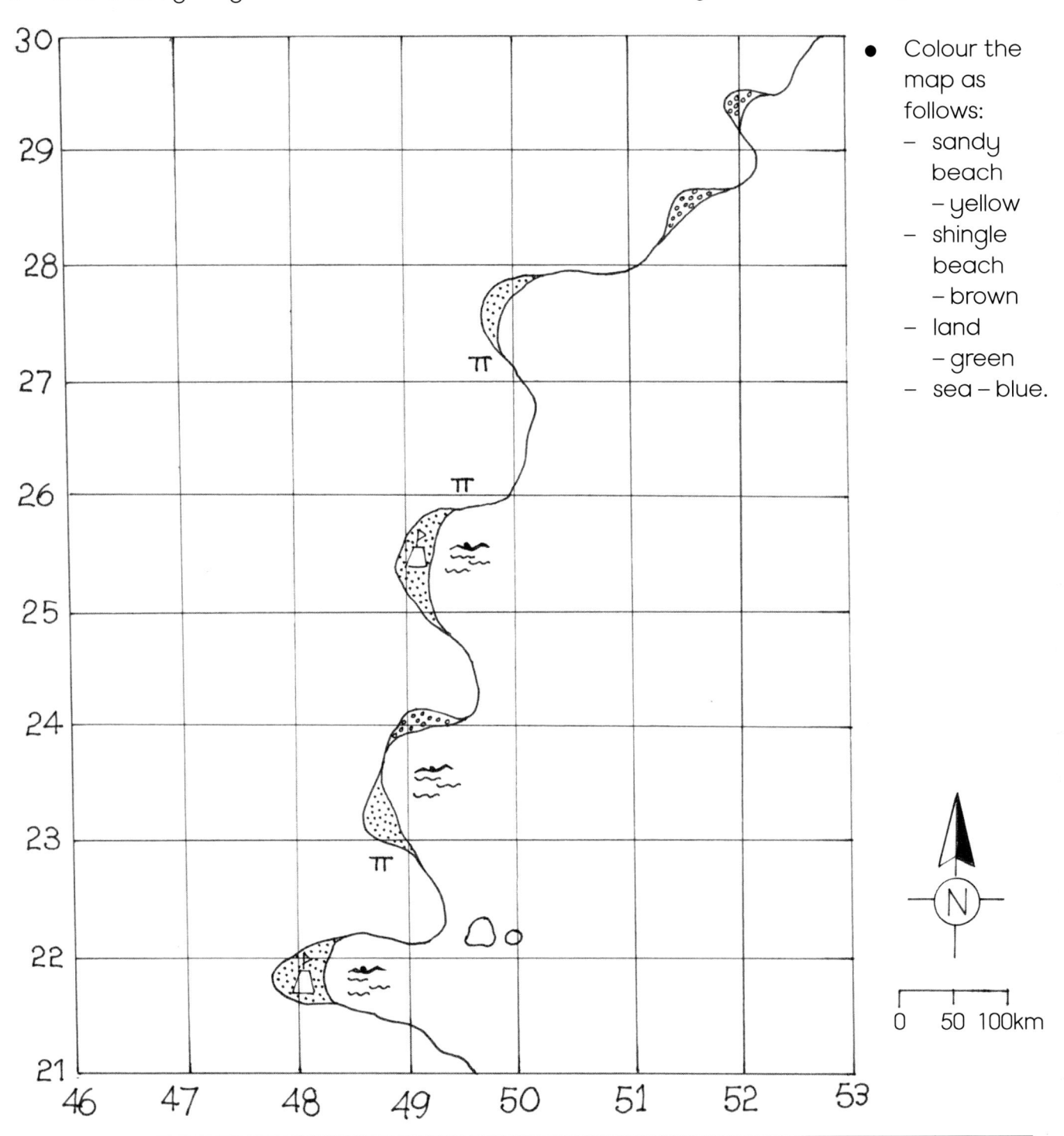

- Colour the map as follows:
  - sandy beach – yellow
  - shingle beach – brown
  - land – green
  - sea – blue.

Beach and activity	Grid reference
sandy beach	_____ _____ _____ _____
shingle beach	_____ _____ _____ _____
sandcastle	_____ _____ _____ _____
swimming	_____ _____ _____ _____
picnic area	_____ _____ _____ _____

© Folens (copiable page) FOLENS GEOGRAPHY IN ACTION 6

Longshore drift

- Look at the diagram and then describe the process of longshore drift.

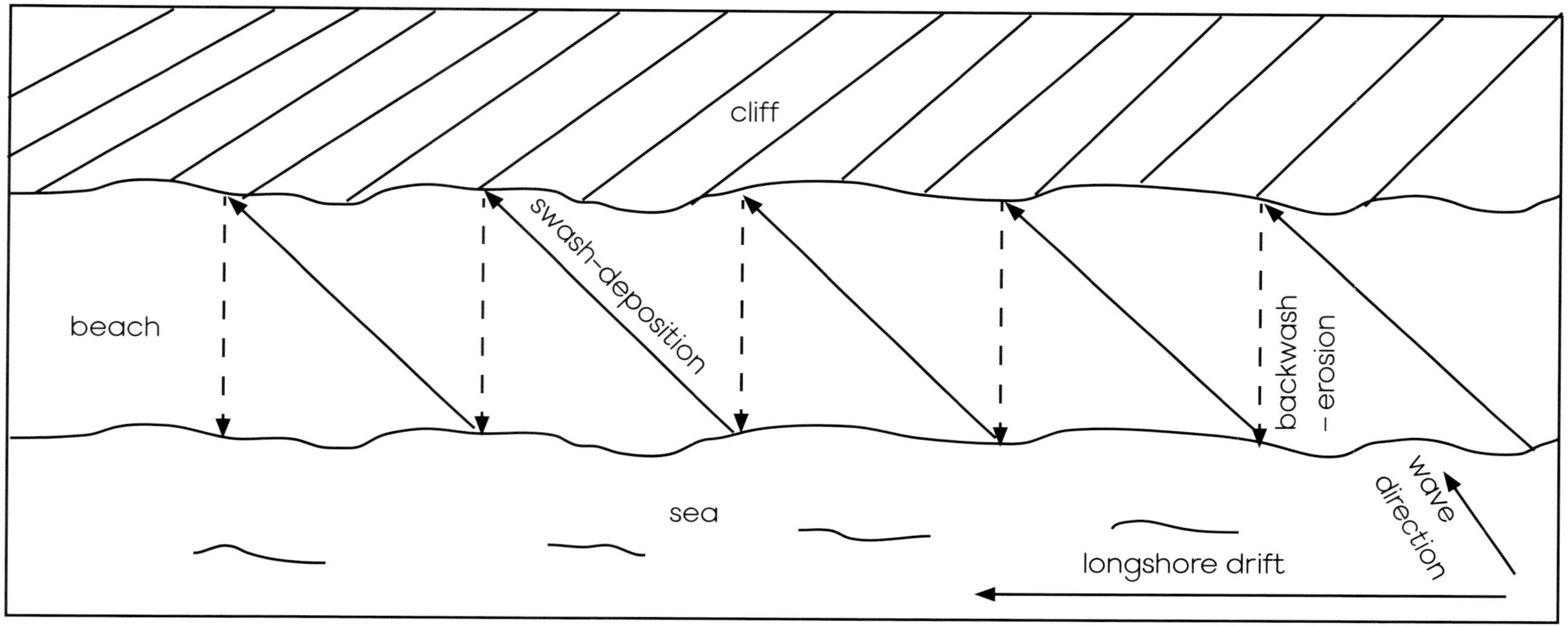

Diagram labels: beach; sea; cliff; swash – deposition; backwash – erosion; longshore drift; wave direction

Longshore drift:
_____
_____
_____
_____

Dune

- Write about a walk from X to Y. Talk about the changing landscape, land use and plant life.

Spurn Head

C10

- In the squared box, draw a map to show the location of Spurn Head. Label the field sketch using the word bank below.

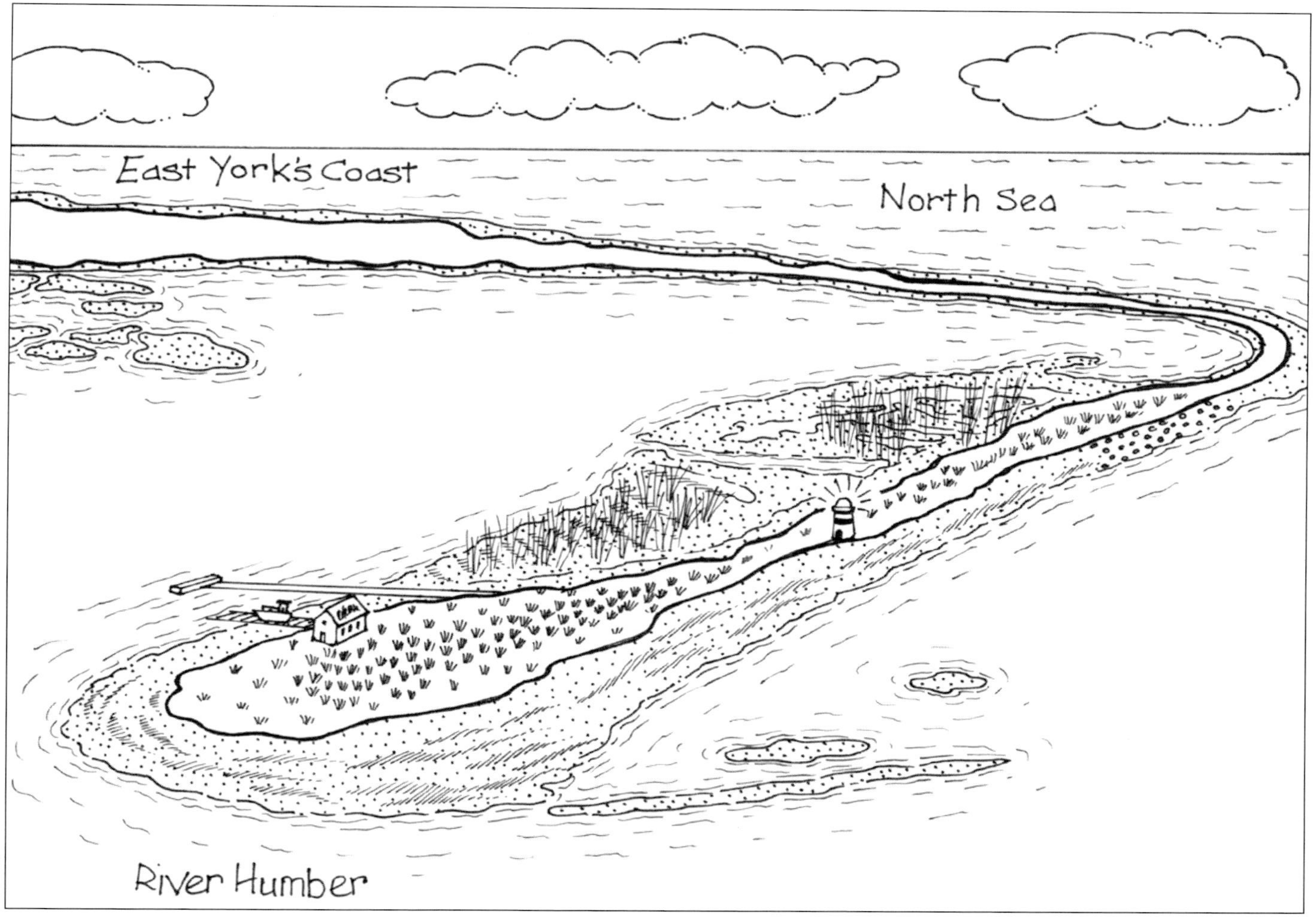

East York's Coast

North Sea

River Humber

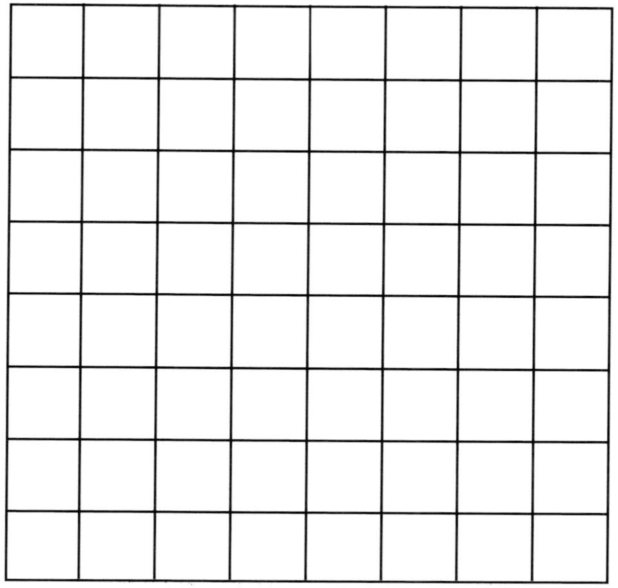

Word bank

5km long	banks
50m wide (narrowest point)	marram grass
reed beds and salt marsh	dunes
lighthouse	sea defences
Humber Estuary	lifeboat station
sand and shingle	mainland

44   FOLENS GEOGRAPHY IN ACTION 6   © Folens (copiable page)

Visiting the Coast

Learning Objectives

Children should:
- learn to ask geographical questions, collect and record evidence and communicate findings in different ways
- locate places and learn about the processes of erosion and deposition that affect coasts.

Background

Each year millions of people visit the coastlines. They go for different reasons, but most go to soak up the sun and enjoy two well-earned weeks relaxing in the sunshine, often guaranteed if they travel abroad. Others enjoy the entertainment that the coastal holiday resorts can offer. In the UK, these may include amusements, gift shops, funfairs and parks, while abroad, there may also be seafront restaurants and bars. On the beach itself, there are other attractions; for children in the UK there will often be donkey rides, Punch and Judy stands, candyfloss and ice cream stalls. The hardy souls who venture out into the cool seas can swim, splash, jet ski or sail. In warmer countries, many people sunbathe or play volleyball, taking the occasional dip to cool off among people swimming, snorkelling, diving or paragliding.

Starting Points	Main Activity	Simplified Activity	Extension Activity
C11 *'Beside the seaside'* Make a list of the activities people may undertake when they are on holiday at the coast.	The activity sheet is a map of a coastal resort showing different activities taking place on and near the beach. Ask the children to give a six-figure grid reference for each activity and the direction and distance to each one from the hotel.	Ask the children to describe the landscape for each activity and give a four-figure grid reference.	Give the children a map, picture or aerial photograph of a stretch of coastline and ask them to mark on suitable places for a variety of activities.
C12 *'Activity holidays'* Together, look at brochures giving details of activity holidays in different parts of the UK and locate some of these places on a wall map or in an atlas.	Ask the children to locate their town on an outline map, then, using a road atlas, plot and describe the routes to the holiday destinations. They should also calculate the distance and time to get to each one.	Ask the children to describe one route to a holiday destination from their home town.	Ask the children to complete a milometer for each journey, starting from and returning to your town after each journey.
C13 *'Birdwatching'* and **C14** *'Rock-climbing'* Together, look at the layout and features of different websites and explore one or two of them in greater depth.	The activity sheets are essentially blank homepages for the children to complete in an attractive style for visitors to the site.	Select either C13 or C14 for the children. Divide the activity sheet into a series of boxes and spaces so that there is a structure to guide them.	Ask the children to produce a further web page to extend their site so that they can give more information about their chosen activity and an itinerary for a week's holiday.

Plenary

Talk to the children about how people spend their leisure time at the coast. Ask individual children to talk about their web pages, the information they contain and to name the type of coastal holiday they would enjoy.

C11

Beside the seaside

- On a separate piece of paper, give a six-figure grid reference for each activity shown on the map. Use the compass and scale to work out the direction and distance to each one from the hotel.

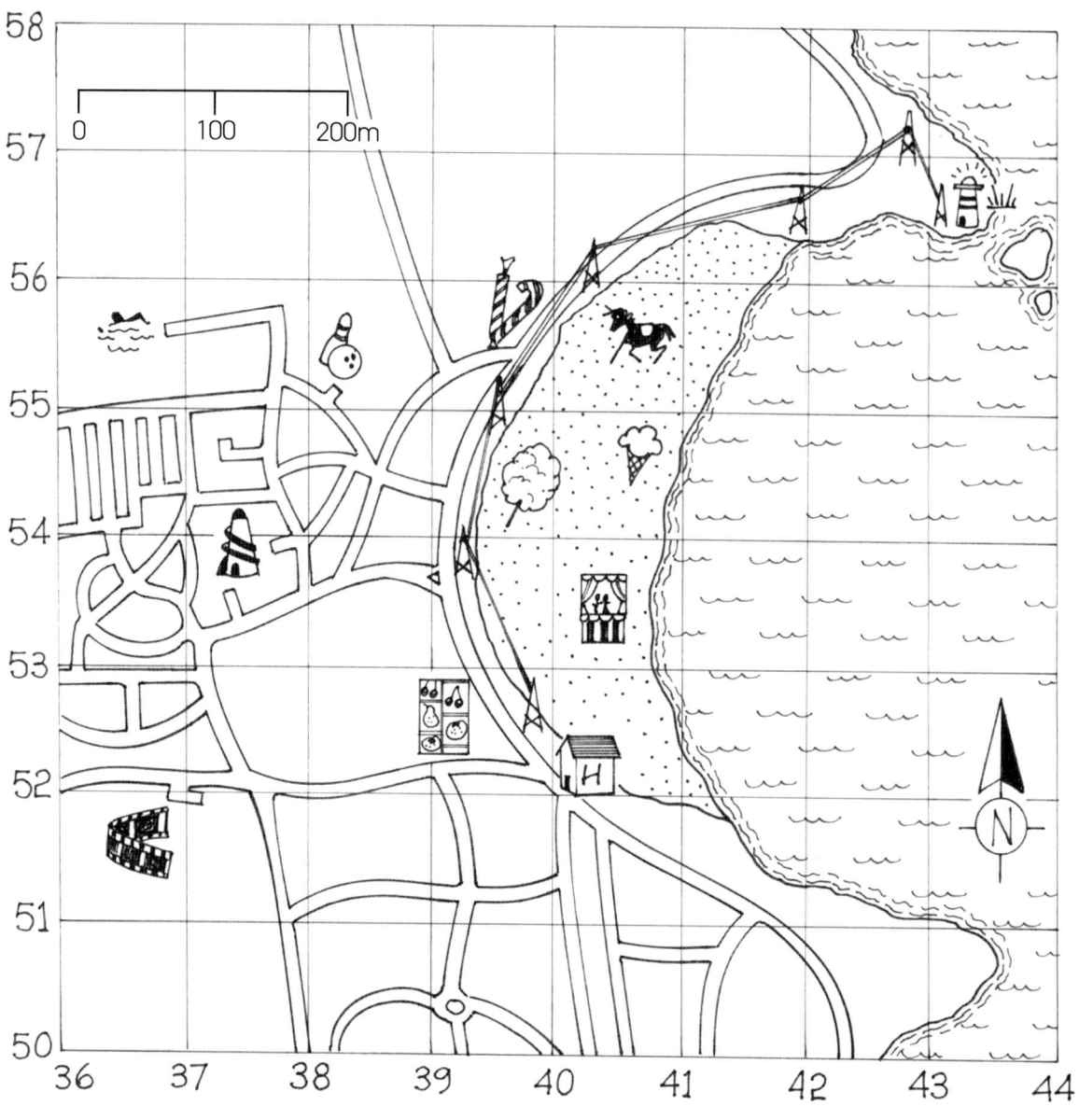

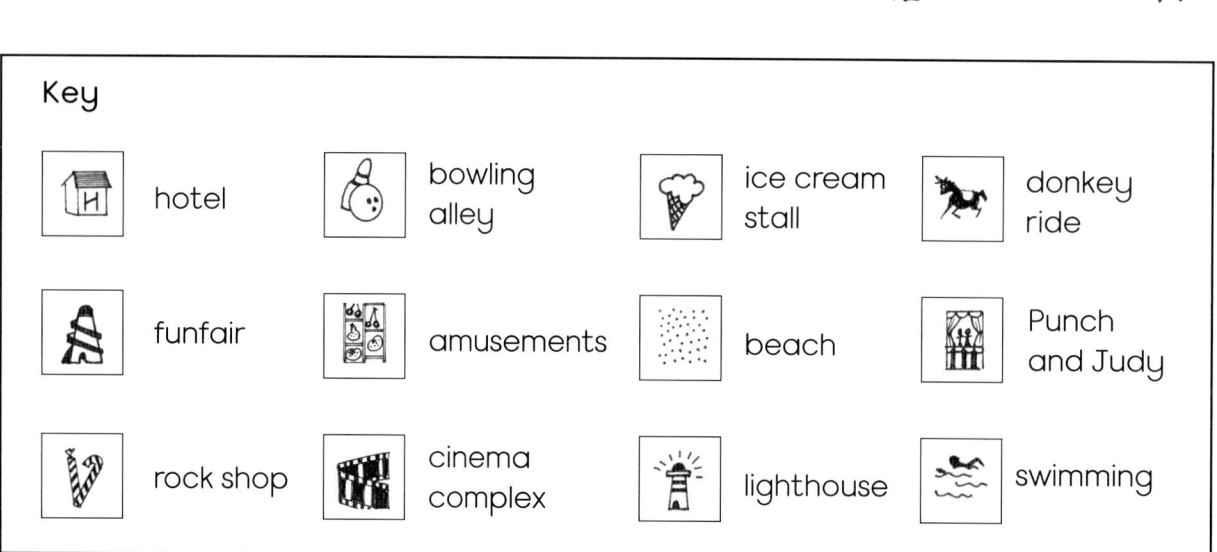

Key

H	hotel
	bowling alley
	ice cream stall
	donkey ride
	funfair
	amusements
	beach
	Punch and Judy
	rock shop
	cinema complex
	lighthouse
	swimming

46 FOLENS GEOGRAPHY IN ACTION 6 © Folens (copiable page)

Activity holidays

C12

- Locate your town on an outline map. Using a road atlas, plot and describe your route to each of the activity holidays. Work out how far each place is and how long it would take you to get there when travelling at 40mph (65kmph). Take a ferry to Northern Ireland.

'Climb in Pembrokeshire'
Scale limestone cliff walls in the southern bays between Solva and St David's Head. B&B at the three-star Hotel Mariners.
1 week in April – £425.

'Winter birds'
See winter birds that flock to our coast at Gibraltar Point in Lincolnshire. Guided walks. Birdwatching weekends in February. Stay at the two-star Vine Hotel.
2 nights – £185.

'A walking tour of Northern Ireland'
Starting at Ballycastle, our base for the week, visit Strangford Lough, the Antrim Glens and Rathin Island, a stopping place for the Vikings over 1000 years ago. Stay at the two-star Fullerton Arms.
1 week in June – £495.

'Soak up the sun in Devon'
Relax in the sun in Torbay on England's Riviera. Stay at the five-star Imperial Hotel, with its 153 bedrooms and luxury suites.
Price on application.

Birdwatching

- Design an attractive Internet page which will encourage people to go birdwatching by the coast. Add images and essential information.

Rock-climbing

- Design an attractive Internet page which will encourage people to go rock-climbing. Add images and essential information.

Features and Land Uses Around the Coast

Learning Objectives

Children should:
- learn to question, collect and record evidence
- learn to use fieldwork techniques
- learn more about coastal features and the processes of erosion and deposition that affect them.

Background

Large-scale OS maps of the part of the coast to be studied will be needed. A 1:25 000 map will show coastal and land use features in greater detail than a 1:50 000. A visit to the coast is an excellent way of introducing the children to different coastal features and land uses. Various fieldwork techniques can be practiced, including field sketching, taking photographs, using and drawing maps, following a trail, using a compass and giving directions and bearings. Check the tides prior to organising the visit.

Some good preliminary work can be done in the classroom before the visit and the skills and techniques learned can then be applied in the field. Allow the children a few minutes to look at OS maps before they are used formally. To direct their attention to a particular part of the map, use a frame which will help them to focus on the section of the coast you wish them to study. Between five and ten kilometres of coast should contain a sufficient number of features.

Starting Points	Main Activity	Simplified Activity	Extension Activity
C15 *'Field sketch'* Using a photograph of a landscape, construct a field sketch, not necessarily coastal, consisting of the major lines of the landscape that roughly outline the features that need to be emphasised. Together, label the field sketch.	Ask the children to point out the main features shown in the drawing and ask them to name the features they should emphasise. They should then draw and label a field sketch on a separate piece of paper.	Make a word bank and attach it to the bottom of the activity sheet. Ask the children to label the field sketch using all of the words.	Hand out copies of images that show coastlines or other landscapes. Give the children two minutes to draw a field sketch of one of them, labelling the main features and land uses.
C16 *'Exploring coastlines'* Look at a large-scale OS map of a coastal area and ask the children to identify features and different land uses.	Ask the children to estimate the direction and distance between each letter on the activity sheet, and note the features and land uses passed as they 'walk' between each one.	Ask the children to look at the map and note the different kinds of land use they can see. They should make a note of them in the order that they are seen on the walk.	Provide a map of a coastal footpath shown on a 1:25 000 OS map. Ask the children to give six-figure grid references to locate the different features and land uses that they encounter on the way.
C17 *'Coastliners'* Show some oblique aerial photographs, preferably of the local area. Ask the children to pick out different land uses.	The activity sheet shows an aerial 'photograph' of a coastal area. Ask the children to identify different land uses and record them on the 'photograph' using appropriate letter codes, for example, H – housing.	On an enlarged copy of the activity sheet, show the children how to join together areas of similar land use and record each use by colouring them with different-coloured highlighter pens. They should include a key.	Ask the children to draw a line from X to Y. Tell them to imagine that they are floating in a hot-air balloon above it. Ask them to write about what they can see directly below as they slowly move across the land.

Plenary

Ask the children to name the land uses found at or near the coast and how they are different to the land uses found around the school.

Field sketch

C15

- Draw a field sketch of this landscape. Label the most important features and land uses.

© Folens (copiable page)   FOLENS GEOGRAPHY IN ACTION 6

Exploring coastlines

- Imagine that you are walking between each letter shown on the map. Record the direction and distance between each letter and note the physical and human features, and land uses you pass on the way. Calculate the total distance.

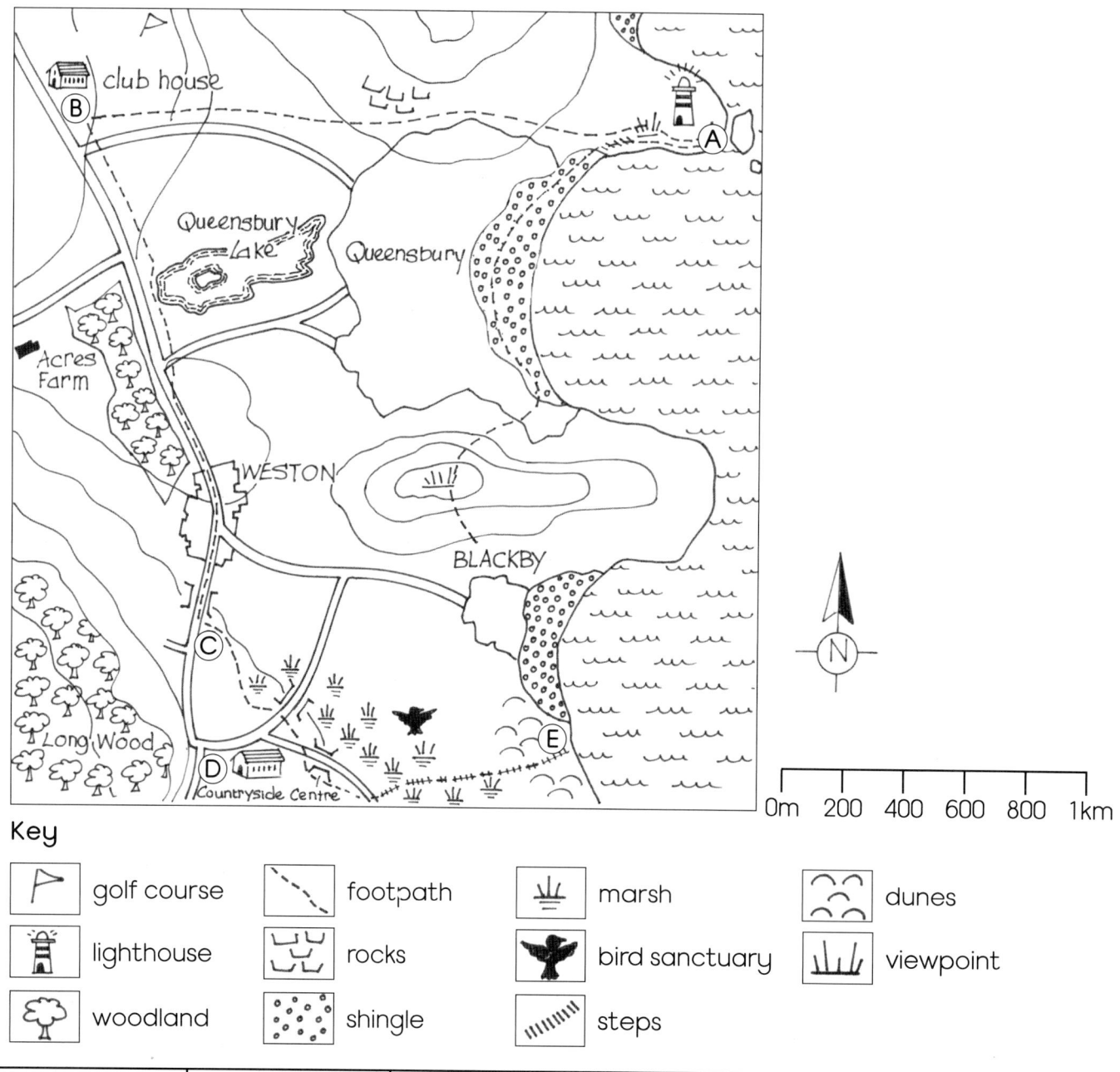

Key

- golf course
- lighthouse
- woodland
- footpath
- rocks
- shingle
- marsh
- bird sanctuary
- steps
- dunes
- viewpoint

	Direction(s)	Distance (km)	Features and land uses passed
A → B			
B → C			
C → D			
D → E			
E → A			

Total distance (km)

FOLENS GEOGRAPHY IN ACTION 6

Coastliners

- Identify different land uses and record them on the aerial 'photograph' below using appropriate letter codes. On a separate piece of paper, make a key.

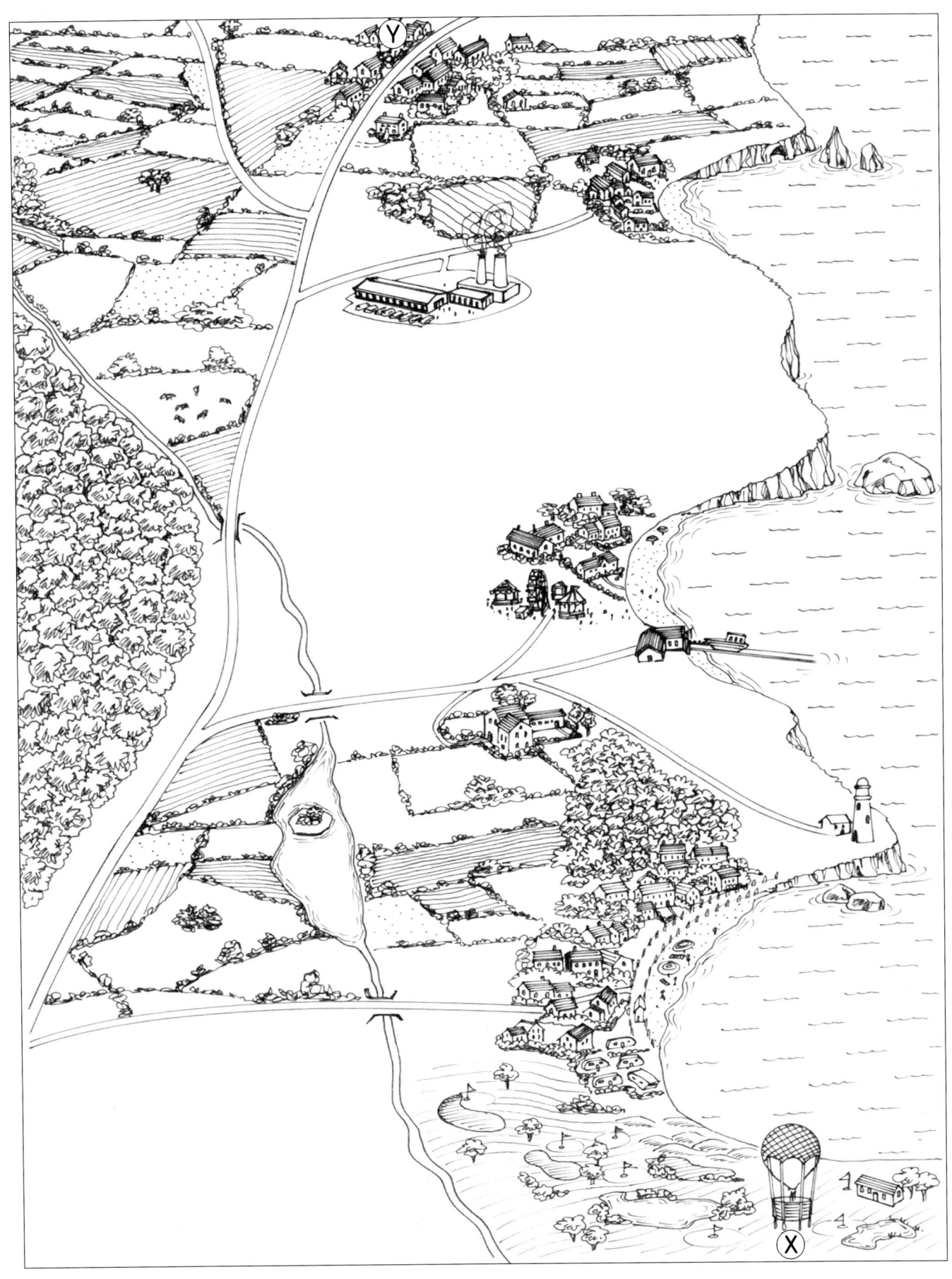

Managing the Coast

Learning Objectives

Children should:
- learn about the physical processes acting on coasts
- learn how and why people may seek to manage environments sustainably.

Background

It is likely that because of global warming, sea levels will rise by over 50cm by the end of this century, that is over five millimetres a year, and that storms will be more frequent and violent. The rise in sea levels will threaten coastal towns, industry, agriculture and some of the most important coastal habitats that are visited by thousands of migrating birds.

Sea defences help protect over 700 000 hectares of land below five metres above sea level. On the north Norfolk coast, several kinds of coastal management are being used, including:
Sea walls – sections of concrete walls that face the sea. They increase erosion immediately in front of the wall, exposing its foundations and increasing the risk of collapse. They therefore have to be replaced approximately every 40 years.
Rock armour – large boulders of hard rock arranged so that large voids are left, thus reducing the energy of breaking waves. The rocks are usually different from local soft rocks so they look out of place.
Groynes – timber piles driven into the beach and connected by a sloping lattice of planks. These do not prevent erosion from taking place but allow sand and shingle to build up behind them.

Starting Points	Main Activity	Simplified Activity	Extension Activity
C18 *'Coastal defence'* Talk about the physical and human issues surrounding coastal erosion.	Together, consider the advantages and disadvantages of the defence schemes shown. Ask the children to label each one and say how each reduces coastal erosion.	Produce a series of statements. Ask the children to cut out the pictures and the statements and stick them together on a piece of A3 paper.	Ask the children to make a labelled wall display showing coastal management schemes. Use blue (sea), yellow (beach) and brown paper to represent the land. Cut out, stick and label the sketches of the different schemes taken from several copies of the activity sheet.
C19 *'Shifting sands'* Talk about how unstable dunes are and that blown sand can damage crops in nearby fields, cars, houses and gardens.	Ask the children to design an area of dune protection which allows public access. The activity sheet provides the children with possible 'fixing' schemes, which can help with their design.	Together, look at the possible 'fixing' schemes and ask the children to suggest where each may be put into practice.	Ask the children to draw and label a map of their management area. Tell them to write questions about the management of dune coasts, such as, 'Why is it important to stabilise dunes?'.
C20 *'Holding back the tide'* Explain that global warming is responsible for melting the polar ice caps and that this will cause sea levels to rise.	Using detailed atlases, ask the children to locate and name some of the towns that may be seriously affected by sea level rises. Colour in the area that may be flooded.	Ask the children to write a brief news article about global warming using a writing frame or software. This should include a headline, spaces for pictures, descriptions and comments from scientists and people who are affected.	Ask the children to find out more about global warming, how it is caused and what the affects may be on our climate. Ask them to give ideas as to how global warming could be reduced.

Plenary

Look again at the effectiveness of the different coastal defence schemes and how sustainable these may be if sea levels continue to rise in the future.

Coastal defence

C18

- Label and describe what each defence scheme looks like. Explain how each scheme reduces coastal erosion, noting the advantages and disadvantages.

C19 Shifting sands

- Create a managed dune coast that people can enjoy. Include public access, a place for a small golf course and hides for birdwatchers. The bullet points below should help you to make decisions.

- Coniferous trees 'fix' very old dunes.
- Bushes 'fix' old dunes.
- Marram grass 'fixes' younger dunes.
- Lengths of decking are used as footpaths over younger (and new) dunes.
- Zigzag fences help stabilise new dunes.
- Marram grass is encouraged to grow inside protective brushwood fences.
- Signs encourage people to be careful and not spoil this fragile environment.

Holding back the tide

- Look at the coastline today and what it could be like at the end of the century. Colour in the area of land that may be flooded. Using an atlas to help, write down the places most at risk.

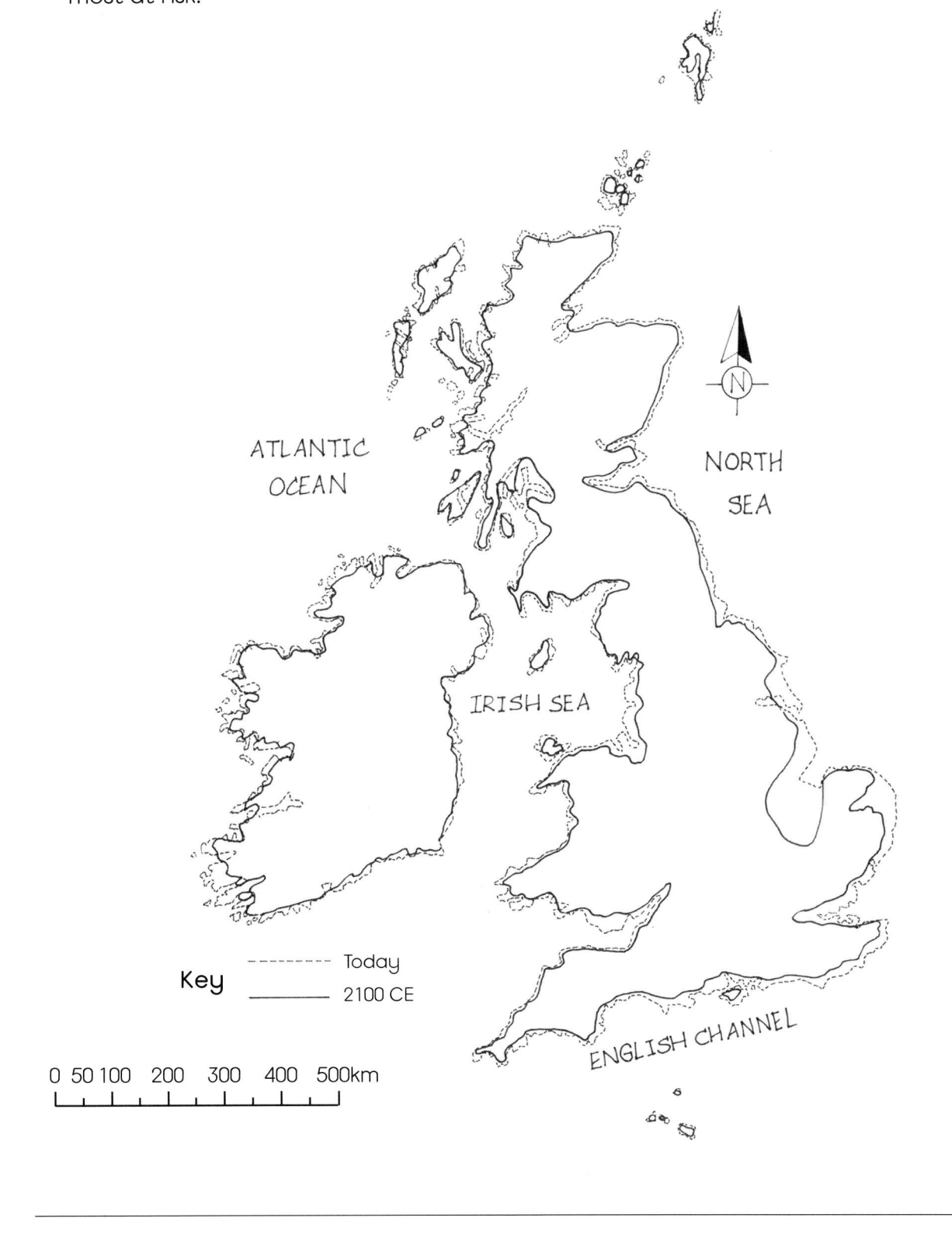

ATLANTIC OCEAN

NORTH SEA

IRISH SEA

ENGLISH CHANNEL

Key
------- Today
———— 2100 CE

0 50 100 200 300 400 500km

Developing the Coast

Learning Objectives

Children should:
- learn that people, including themselves, hold different views about geographical issues
- learn how decisions about places and environments affect the future quality of people's lives.

Background

Large-scale developments in unspoilt, picturesque areas will always attract debate and opinion from a range of interest groups, whether the development is concerned with building a road, a racetrack or a leisure facility on the coast. This part of the children's work needs to focus on the different views people have with regards to developments in their locality and the reasons for them. It will involve the children interpreting photographs and maps. Encourage them to make informed decisions and judgements.

Starting Points	Main Activity	Simplified Activity	Extension Activity
C21 *'Truffles Hotel'* Ask the children to suggest the advantages and disadvantages of a new hotel complex being built on the coast and say who would benefit and who would lose out.	Ask the children to cut out the plan of the hotel complex and place it in different positions on the map, being careful to find the best site for the hotel, with a sea view, while causing the least disruption for local people. They should note the advantages and disadvantages of the site they choose.	Place the hotel in one position. Ask the children to look at the advantages and disadvantages of locating the hotel in that place.	Encourage the children to draw a picture of this section of the coast from Dolphin Island or Trigger Island. They should include various physical and human features and label them.
C22 *'For or against?'* Ask the children to think about and name the groups who would like or dislike a new hotel to be built.	Ask the children to write a short statement for each group on the activity sheet, outlining the views that may be used in a public enquiry.	Give the children a small list of people and groups who may be directly affected by the building of a hotel. Ask them to think of the view each may have and why they may hold these views.	Ask the children to make a list of all the interested parties including those shown on the activity sheet and others. Ask them to rank these views in order of importance.
C23 *'Labels'* Make a large speech bubble for each group and give each a label from the activity sheet. Use the blank label to add another group that the children think should be included. Complete each speech bubble after asking the children questions and gaining a consensus of opinion from them.	The activity sheet is an information sheet containing labels to be used in a public enquiry. The children should debate the issues in small groups, adopting the roles of chairperson, hotel owner, local resident, rambler and holidaymaker.		

Plenary

Tell the children to vote for or against the development in a secret ballot.

Truffles Hotel

C21

- Cut out and decide upon a location for Truffles Hotel by placing it onto the map. Note the advantages and disadvantages of each site and stick the hotel in the best site. Say why you have chosen your site.

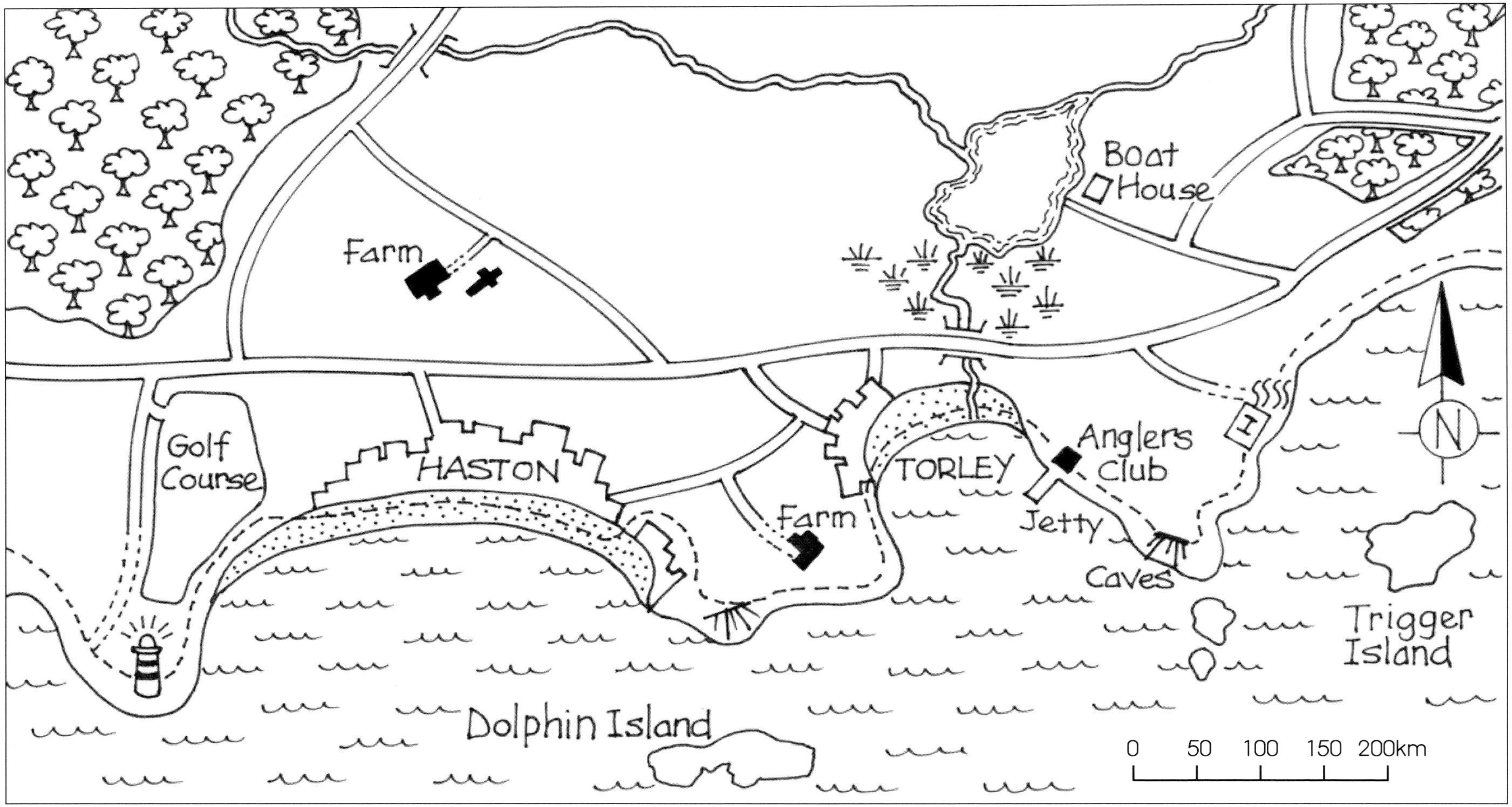

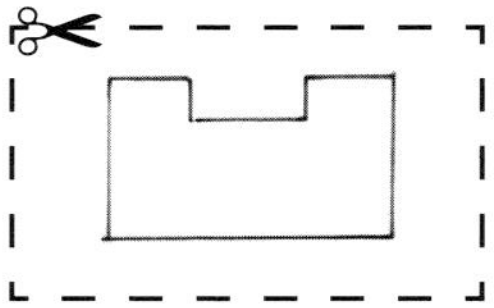

For or against?

- Write a short statement from each group for the Board of Enquiry to consider regarding Truffles Hotel. Think of another interested group, draw them and add a label and a statement from them.

Hotel owner

Statement to the Board of Enquiry
_____
_____
_____
_____

Statement to the Board of Enquiry
_____
_____
_____
_____

Local residents

Rambler

Statement to the Board of Enquiry
_____
_____
_____
_____

Statement to the Board of Enquiry
_____
_____
_____
_____

Holidaymaker

Statement to the Board of Enquiry
_____
_____
_____
_____

Labels

| Chairperson |

| Hotel owner |

| Local residents |

| Rambler |

| Holidaymaker |

| Public enquiry |

| |

Different Kinds of Rain

Learning Objective

Children should:
- learn about the water cycle, including condensation and evaporation.

Background

Rain is droplets of water greater than one millimetre in diameter, which fall to the earth; smaller droplets float in the air as mist or fog. The UK receives rain all the year round as convectional rain, frontal rain and relief rain. Convectional rain occurs typically in the late afternoon as late summer downpours, sometimes accompanied by thunder and lightning. It is caused by the sun warming the ground and causing moist air to rise; as it rises the moist air cools, condenses and falls as rain. Frontal rain is brought in on the border between warm and cold air. Under these conditions, warm air is pushed over the cold air and as a result, the air on its leading edge cools, condenses and rain falls. Frontal rain can take several hours to pass over. Relief rain falls when moist air is forced to rise over highland, again cooling and condensing to form rain. Most rain in the UK falls as frontal or relief rain
and areas of higher land, on the western side of the country facing the prevailing wind, receive the most.

Starting Points	Main Activity	Simplified Activity	Extension Activity
R1 *'Every time it rains'* Tell the children about the different kinds of rain that the UK receives and make a collection of words that describe them, such as drizzle and downpour, on the flip chart.	Discuss the different ways that the UK receives its rainfall. Using bullet points, ask the children to describe each process in the box next to the diagram.	Explain the processes carefully and clearly to the children and, in pairs or with an adult, ask them to explain one of the ways in which the UK receives its rainfall.	Ask the children to research vocabulary for rainfall and to produce a rainfall glossary using reference books and the Internet.
R2 *'Rainfall map'* Show the children a physical wall map of the UK that has highland and lowland areas of the country. Talk about the prevailing westerly wind that brings most of our rain across the Atlantic.	Discuss the distribution of rainfall across the UK. Ask the children to write a short paragraph describing the pattern of rainfall across the UK.	Ask the children to write short notes about where the high and low rainfall areas are located.	Using an atlas, ask the children to locate a town in a high rainfall area and another in a dry area and mark them on the map. Ask them to research the weather that each receives and to draw graphs to show the information they have collected and compare them.
R3 *'Water cycle'* Draw a large diagram on the board and describe the process of the water cycle to the children, ensuring that all of its components are discussed in turn. (Shape order: sun, evaporation, condensation, clouds, prevailing wind, clouds move inland, clouds rise to cool, water droplets merge, rain falls, streams and rivers return water to the sea.)	Ask the children to list in the word bank the words used to describe the distinct components of the water cycle in order. Add to each half of a shape a word in the bank. Cut out the shapes and stick them onto plain paper to show the water cycle. Add a title.	Complete the word bank and half of each shape for the children. Ask them to finish the shapes and stick them onto plain paper in the correct order.	Ask the children to draw the water cycle as a cross-section, labelling all of the components within it.

Plenary

Ask some of the children to describe the different ways that the UK receives its rain and where most of it falls and why it falls there. Using the large diagram on the whiteboard, ask some of the children to describe the water cycle using labelled sticky notes.

Every time it rains

R1

- Use bullet points to describe each of the ways we receive rainfall. The numbers on each diagram will help you.

Convectional rain

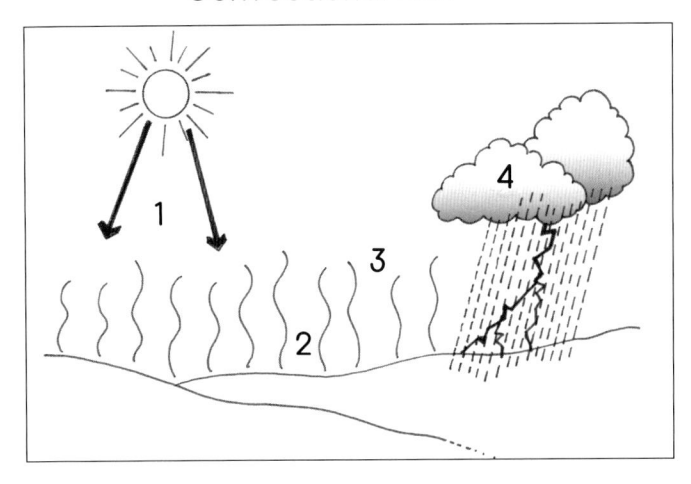

Frontal rain

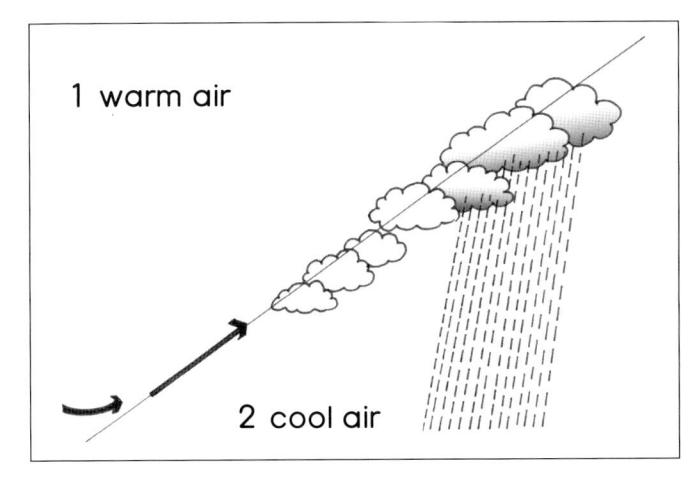

1 warm air

2 cool air

Relief rain

© Folens (copiable page)   FOLENS GEOGRAPHY IN ACTION 6   63

Rainfall map

- Look at the map below and write a short description about the pattern of rainfall across the United Kingdom.

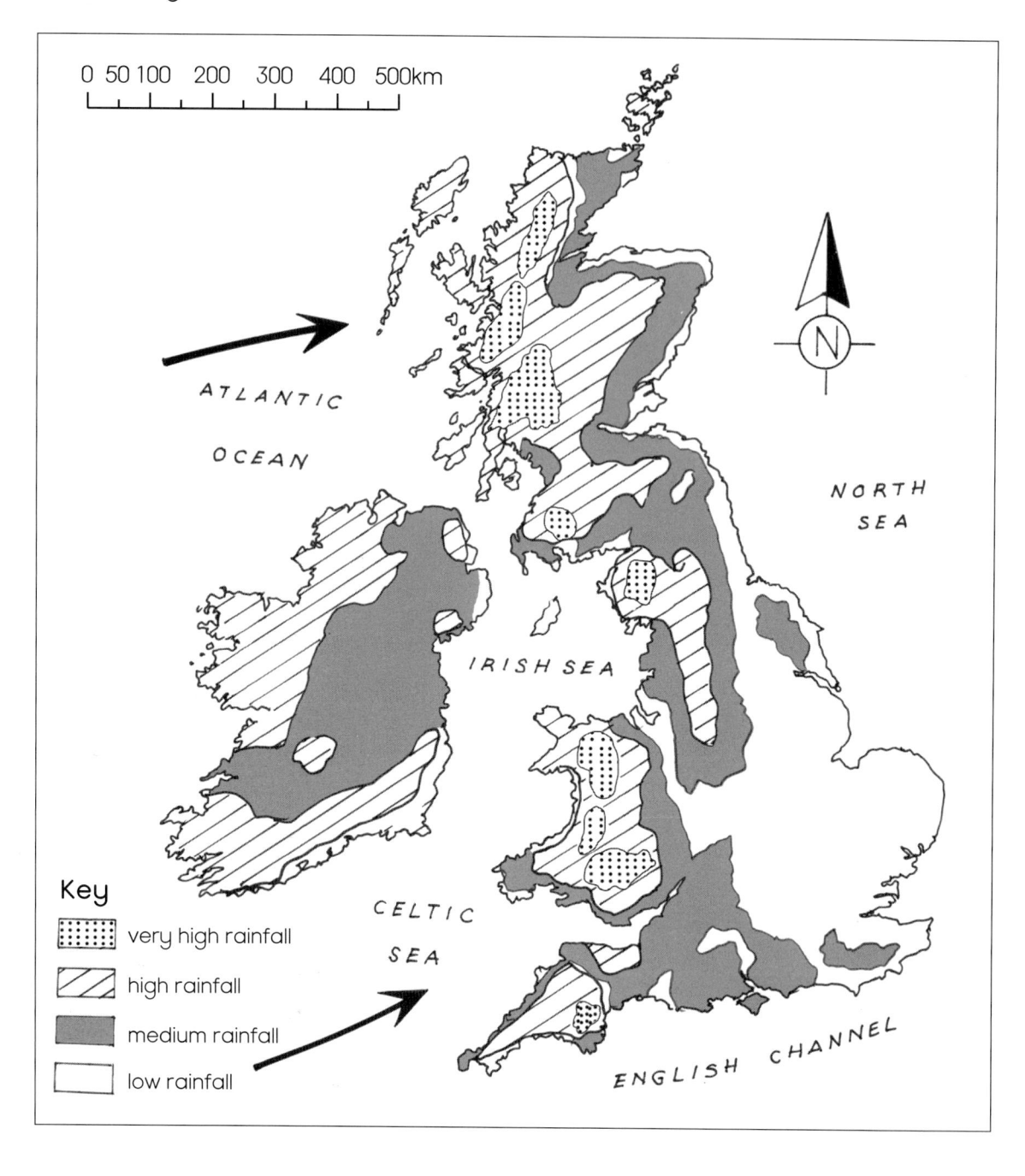

Key
- very high rainfall
- high rainfall
- medium rainfall
- low rainfall

R3

Water cycle

- Complete the word bank and then the shapes to create a water cycle. One has been begun for you. Cut out the shapes, stick them in order (writing one word in each half of a shape) to show the water cycle. Add a title to the diagram.

sun

Word bank

sun

© Folens (copiable page)   FOLENS GEOGRAPHY IN ACTION 6   65

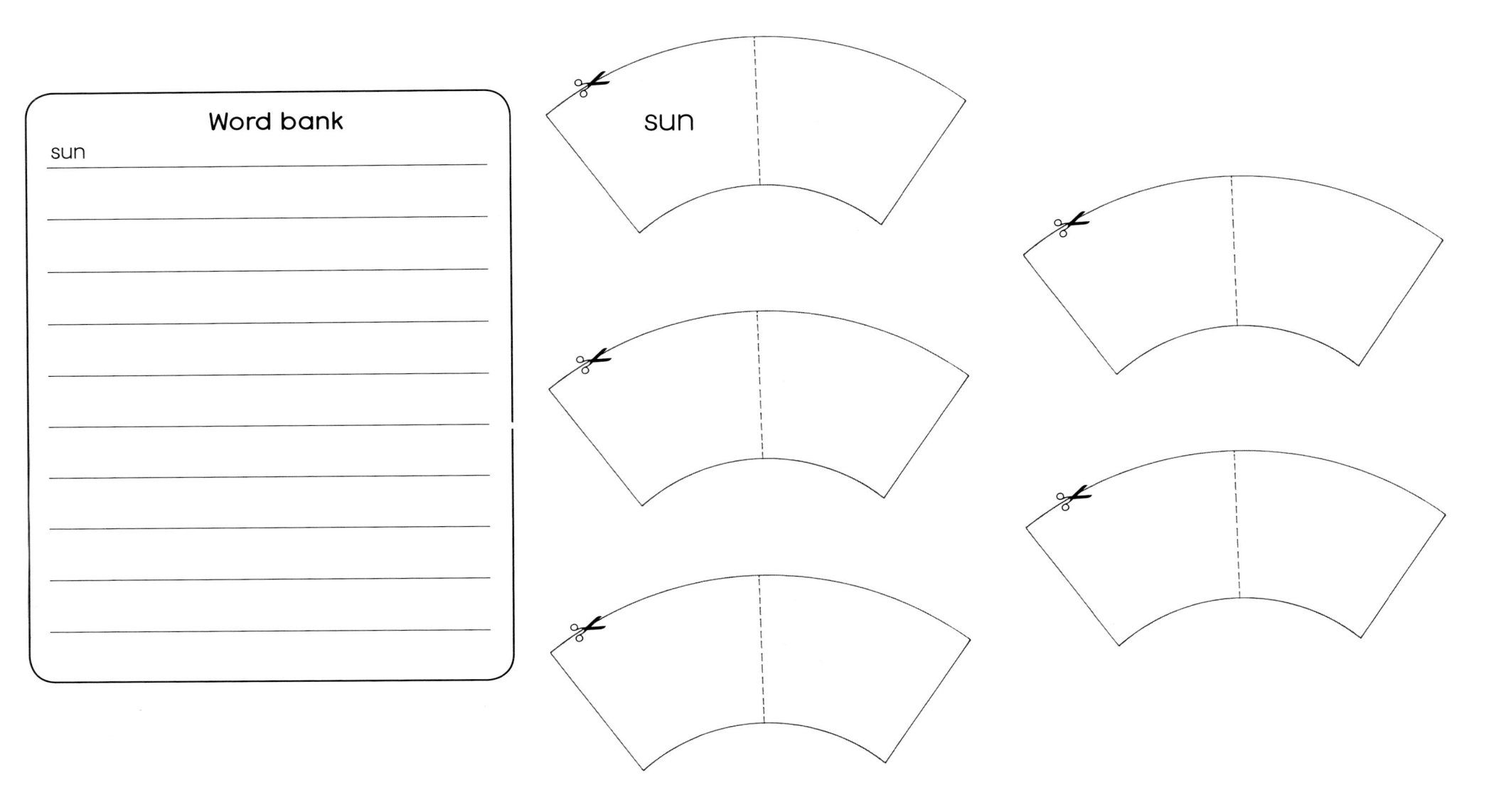

Water Around the School

Learning Objective

Children should:
- learn about how site conditions can influence the weather.

Background

There is a large element of fieldwork in this section; most of the activities and investigations described here can be undertaken around the school grounds. Look for water run-off and collection areas where puddles may form after rain, mark them on a base map of the school and take photographs of these areas to use in school. It is useful before beginning any work with the children to look at a plan of the school and its grounds and spend some time naming the different areas and places within it. It is important that the children have some understanding of the different elements of the weather and how they combine to form the conditions being experienced at any time.

Starting Points	Main Activity	Simplified Activity	Extension Activity
R4 *'Micro-climate'* Give out copies of a plan of your school. Talk about the different weather elements and how local site conditions may affect each of them. Discuss the movement of the sun throughout the day.	Talk about the specific characteristics of location A using the data chart. Ask the children to look at the micro-climate at the other locations and predict the weather data they might collect at each point at the same time of day.	Ask the children to note the individual site characteristics of each location with a partner.	Ask the children to justify and explain their predictions.
R5 *'Water, water everywhere'* Explain what puddles are, how they are formed and where they can usually be found in the school grounds.	Ask the children to locate each 'photograph' and say where else, by looking at the intervals between the contours, water may collect.	Take the children into the school grounds, preferably after heavy rain and, with the plan of your school, locate the places where rainwater collects.	Ask the children to place a metre-squared grid divided into 10cm intervals over a puddle and map the puddle onto one centimetre-squared graph paper, noting the time. Calculate its area. Calculate the new area at 15-minute intervals.
R6 *'Map making'* Talk about water movement features found on plans of the school grounds. Explain how these plans can be made accurately.	Put the children into small groups and ask them to follow the instructions on the sheet. The more points recorded around the feature, the more accurate the finished map will be. (A teacher and an assistant should try this first to demonstrate to the children.)		
R7 *'Measuring puddles'* Talk about how puddles evaporate over time.	Ask pairs of children to add a measured amount of water to some cotton wool and then weigh it. Place these in different locations outside for about 15 minutes each time and weigh again. Record the starting weight and weight loss for each period due to evaporation.	Help the children to conduct the investigation. They can use a calculator to determine weight loss.	Ask the children to rank weather conditions according to the rates of evaporation each would give, starting with the one that would produce the highest rate.

Plenary

Talk about the site of your school and how the micro-climate varies around the grounds. Ask the children to conclude where the sunniest, warmest and windiest places are and where most evaporation will occur after heavy rain.

Micro-climate

R4

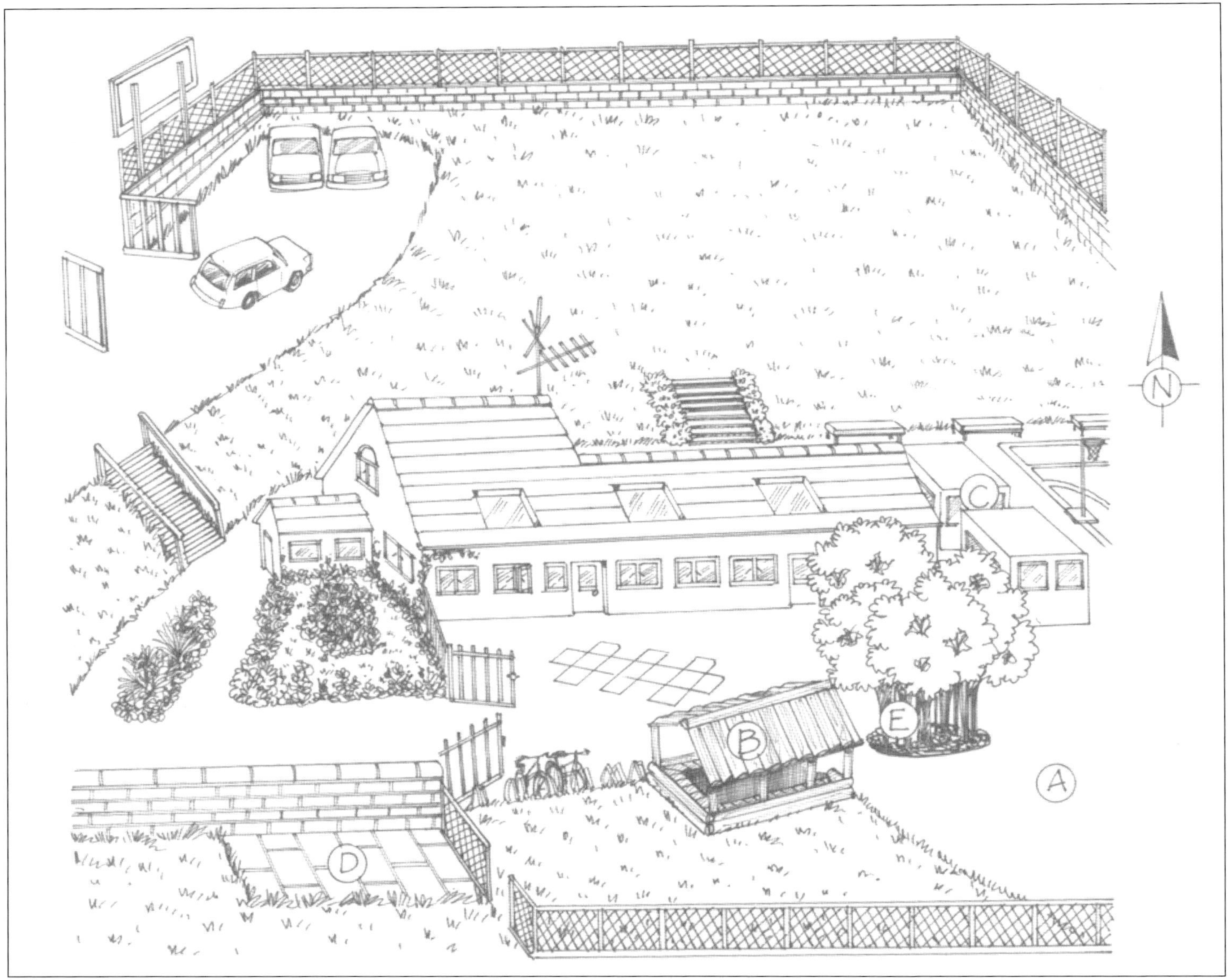

- Look at the field sketch and label the different features. Examine the micro-climate data collected at location A. Predict the data you might collect at the other locations at the same time of day and complete the chart below.

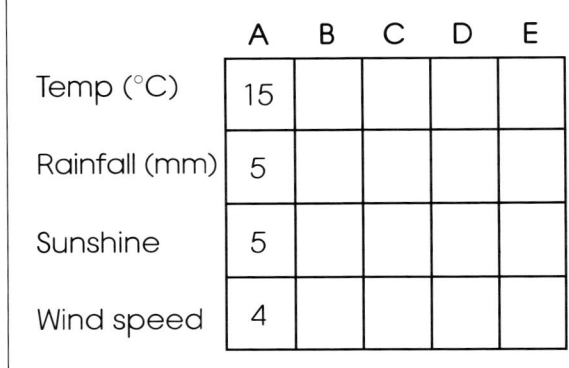

	A	B	C	D	E
Temp (°C)	15				
Rainfall (mm)	5				
Sunshine	5				
Wind speed	4				

(Mark temperature in °C. Score all others between 0, low, to 5, high.)

© Folens (copiable page)

FOLENS GEOGRAPHY IN ACTION 6

Water, water everywhere

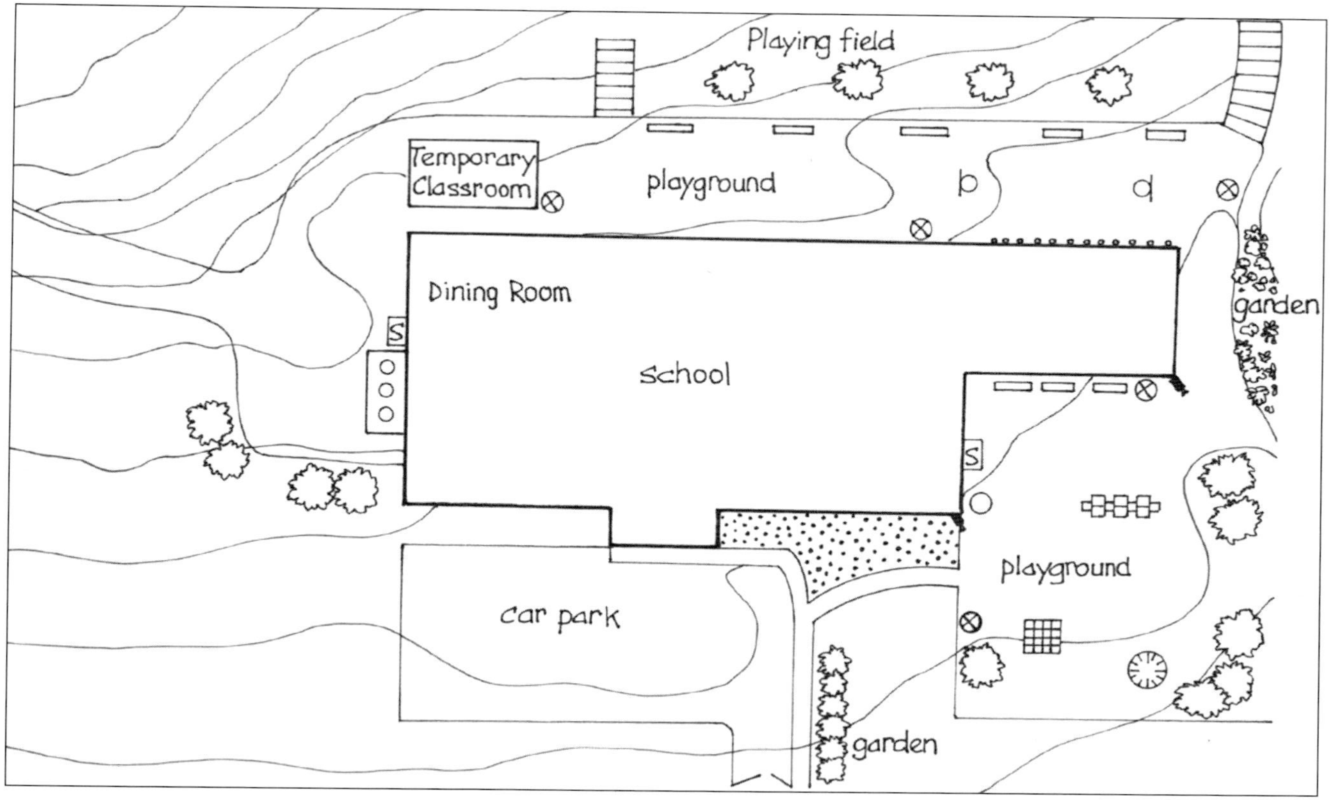

R5

- Look at the contour lines and the 'photographs'. Mark on the map the position at which each 'photograph' was taken. Find another place where a puddle may form, draw a picture of it and indicate on the plan where it was taken from.

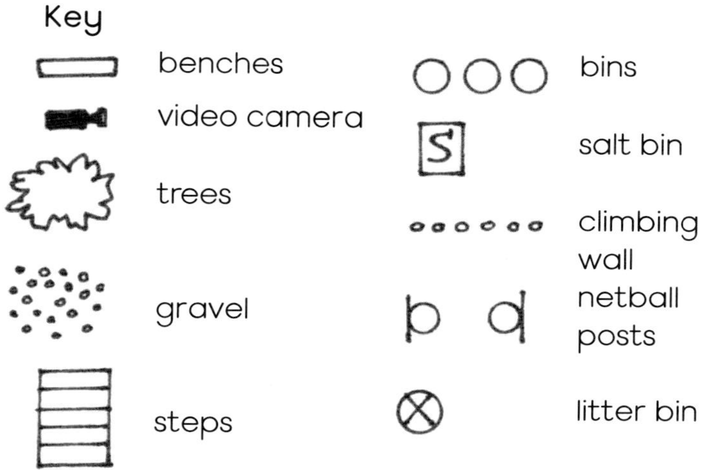

Key

- ◯◯◯ bins
- 🅂 salt bin
- ∘∘∘∘∘ climbing wall
- p netball posts
- ⊗ litter bin
- 🮶 video camera
- ❀ trees
- ⋯ gravel
- ▦ steps

'Photograph' 1

'Photograph' 2

'Photograph' 3

'Photograph' 4

68   FOLENS GEOGRAPHY IN ACTION 6   © Folens (copiable page)

Map making

R6

- Make a map of some features in your school grounds using the method below. Try to include some water features.

1. Choose an area to map containing a variety of features.
2. Stretch a measuring tape vertically over the area.
3. Place a metre stick along the base of the tape at right angles.
4. Attach two pieces of A4 graph paper together to make a long strip.
5. Draw a vertical line on the left-hand side of the paper to represent the measuring tape and a horizontal line at the bottom to represent a metre stick. (Use an appropriate scale.)
6. Move the metre stick along the tape at right angles.
7. When a feature is reached, mark the co-ordinates created on the graph paper.
8. Repeat for each point of the feature reached.

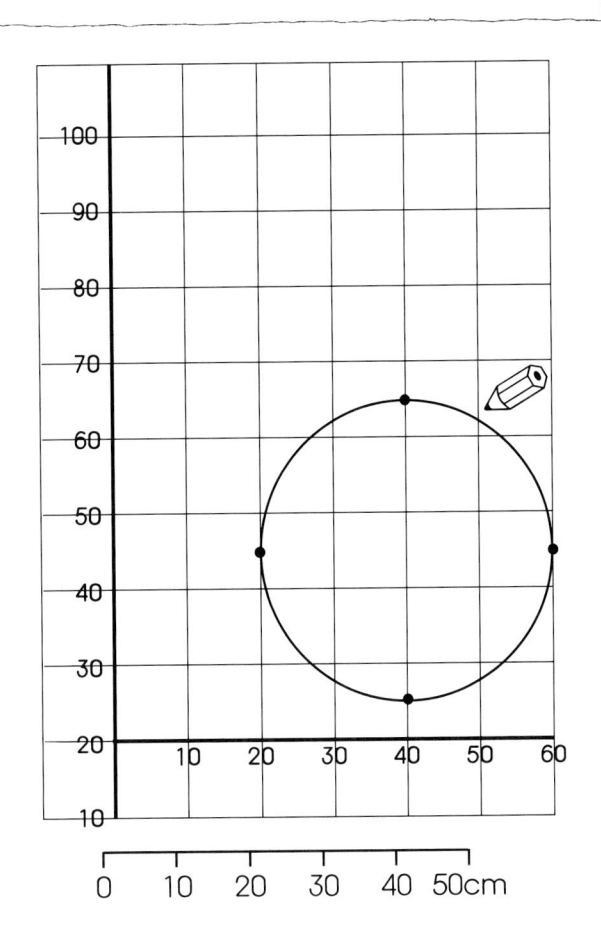

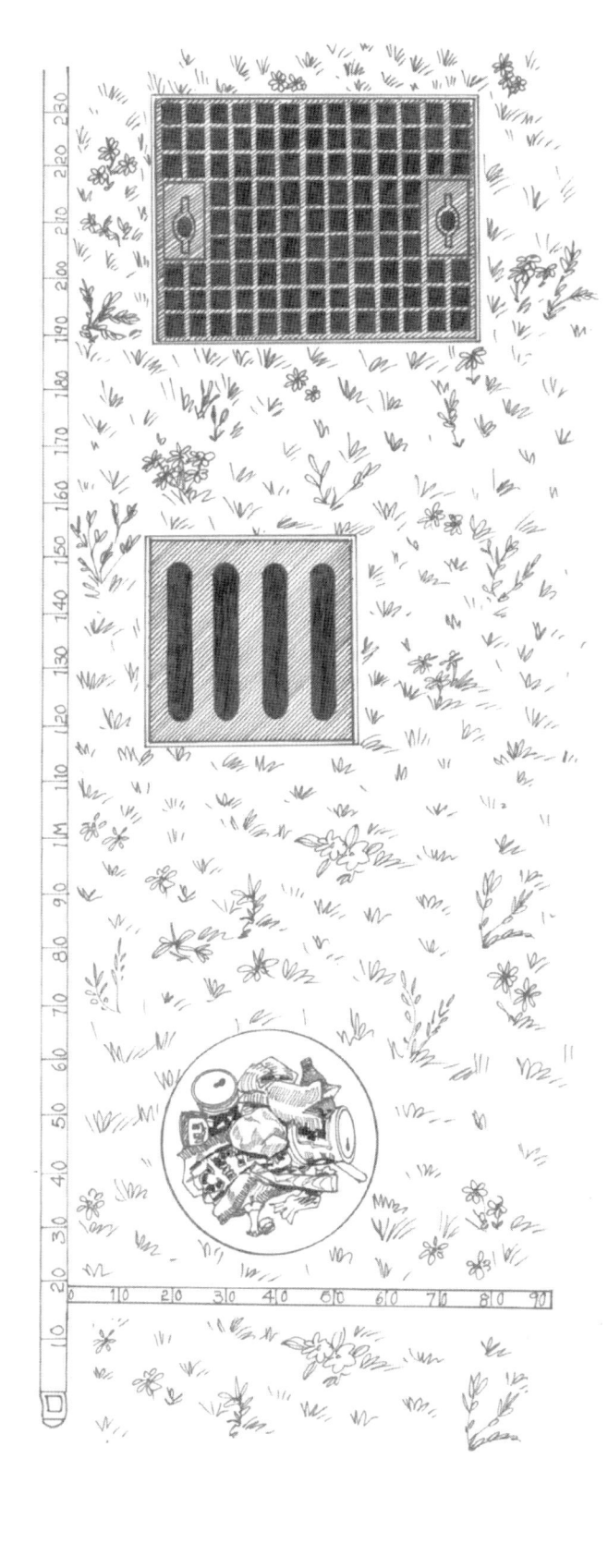

© Folens (copiable page)   FOLENS GEOGRAPHY IN ACTION 6

R7

Measuring puddles

- Carry out an investigation to find out where in your school grounds rates of evaporation are highest. Write in the boxes below.

Method:

1. Description: _____
   _____

2. Description: _____
   _____

   weight _____ g

Location 1 – where and weather	→	starting weight (g)	weight loss (g)
Location 2 – where and weather	→	starting weight (g)	weight loss (g)
Location 3 – where and weather	→	starting weight (g)	weight loss (g)

What I found out …

_____
_____
_____
_____
_____

Rivers in the Landscape

Learning Objectives

Children should:
- learn to undertake fieldwork
- learn how rivers erode, transport and deposit materials producing particular landscape features.

Background

Fieldwork is a good way of introducing the children to river features and processes. Streams are more immediate to them because they are smaller, safer, easier to map and cross if needed. Children will be able to see a greater variety of features over a much shorter distance and it may even be possible for the children to walk from the source of the stream to the point at which it joins another stream or river. They will be able to get close to areas of erosion and deposition, rapids, waterfalls and pools, and walk around the course of a meander in a matter of seconds rather than the 10 or 15 minutes it might take if they studied a river.

⚠️ Look for hazards, areas of potential danger and nearby land use. Check to find out who owns the land and ask permission to be on it well before the planned visit date.

Starting Points	Main Activity	Simplified Activity	Extension Activity
R8 *'Go with the flow'* Tell the children how rivers and streams are shown on OS maps and ask them to find some on local maps.	Look at the features shown on the right of the activity sheet. Discuss each one. Tell the children to look carefully for evidence as to where the features might be. The dots mark the position of a feature.	Provide the children with pre-labelled features to cut out and stick to the map.	Ask the children to find out more about the river features shown on the activity sheet and how rivers transport and erode material.
R9 and **R10** *'Information stream (1) and (2)'* Talk to the children about a field visit to a local stream and about the tasks they will complete when there. At the stream, take photographs to record the children at work and talk about land use.	When joined, the activity sheets form a sketch of a section of a stream and data collected about it; the same type of information should be collected on the field visit. Ask the children to draw a map of the stream on A3 paper.	Produce an outline map of the stream for the children to complete.	Ask the children to draw a cross-section of the stream bed along the depths marked and label the deep and shallow parts of the stream.
R11 *'Mapping streams'* Look at OS maps and note how contour lines, especially those that cross streams, bend and point to the stream's source.	On the first map, ask the children to draw in the network of rivers and tributaries the contours suggest should be there. On the second map, they should draw in the contour lines they would expect to see if this was drawn on an OS map.	Ask the children to complete the first map only and look particularly at the V-shaped contours that indicate the presence of a stream.	Ask the children to attempt to draw the drainage basin of a small stream system using an extract of a 1:50 000 or 1:25 000 OS map. A drainage basin is an area of hillside that is drained to a network of streams that flow into each other. They should look out for the ridge of land that will divide different basins.

Plenary

Explain how rivers affect the landscape and how maps record this. Ask the children to give their views and feelings about the stream they visited or studied and make a list of the words they use.

R8

Go with the flow

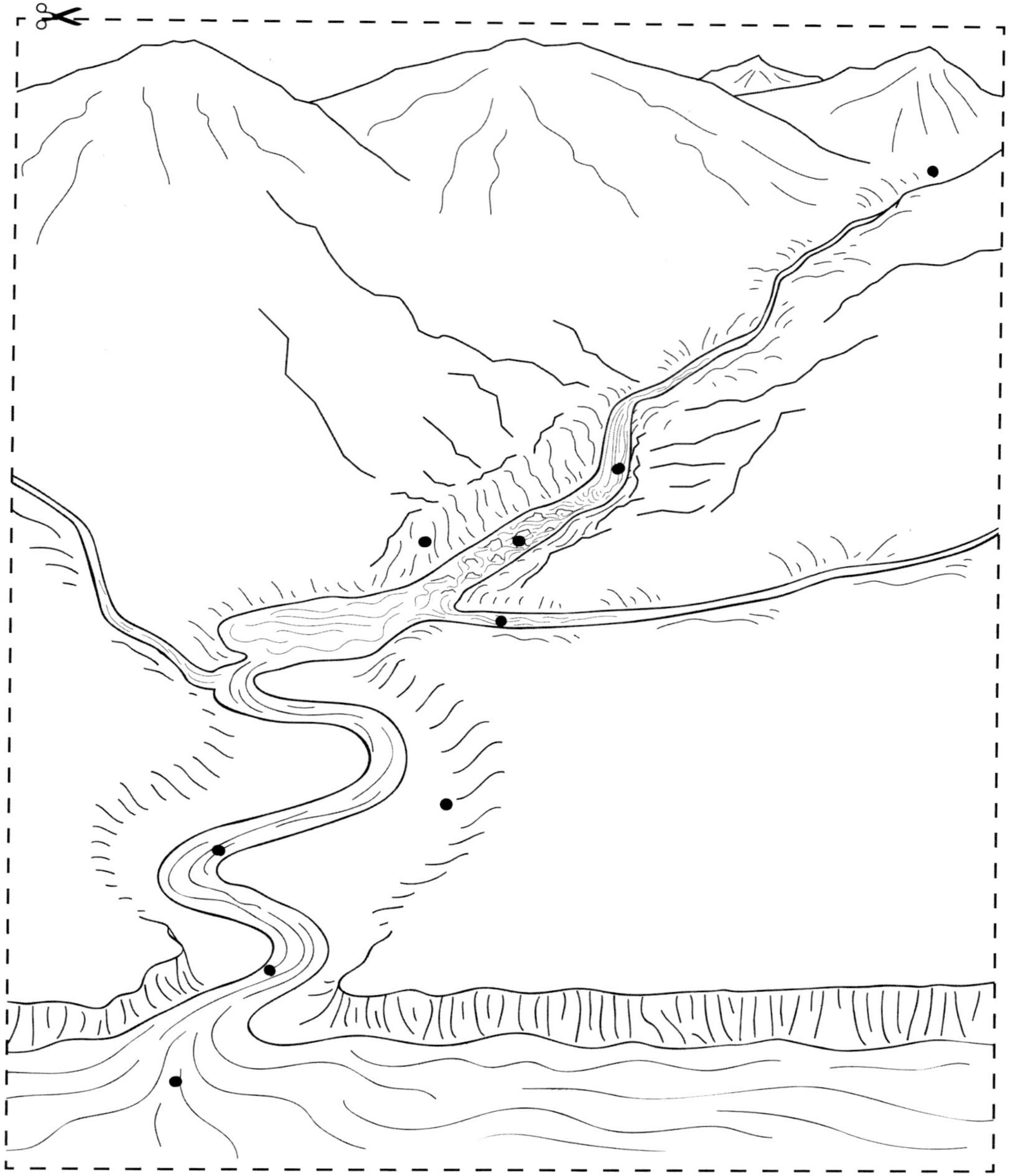

- Label each feature using the word bank. Cut out and stick the map onto an A3 sheet of paper and then link each of the features to the correct dot on the map.

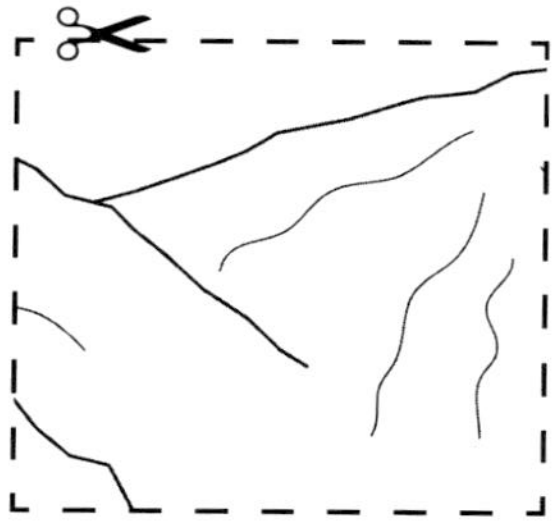

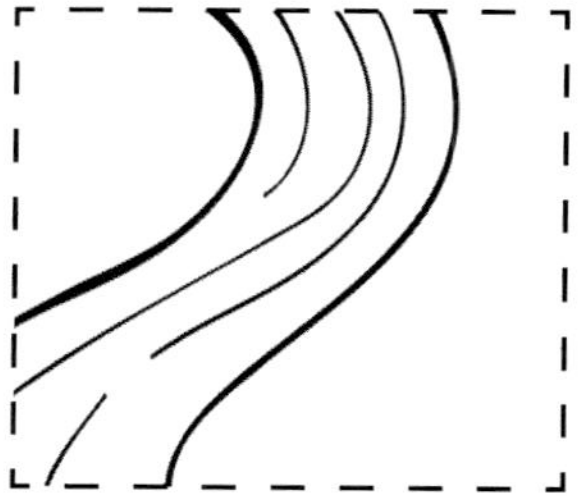

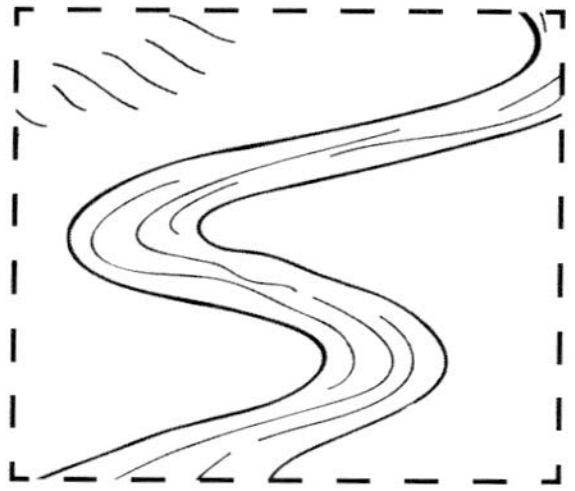

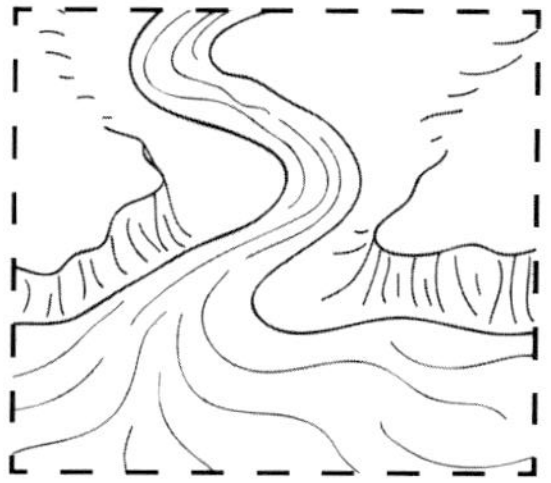

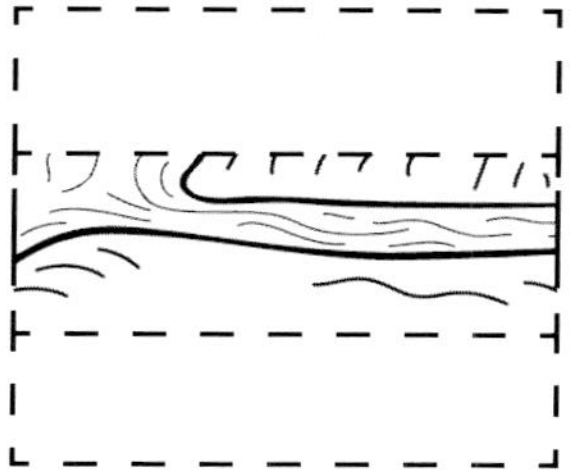

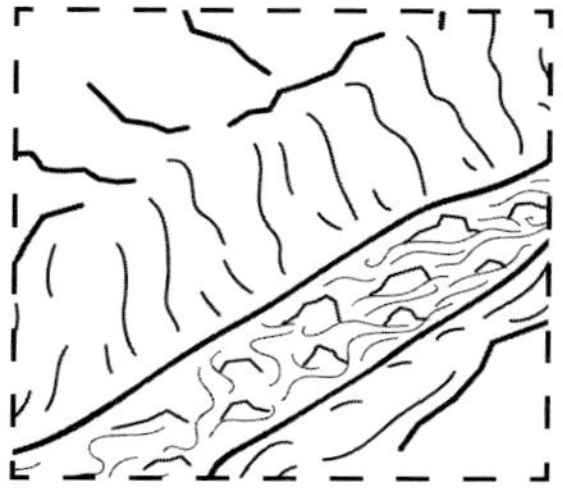

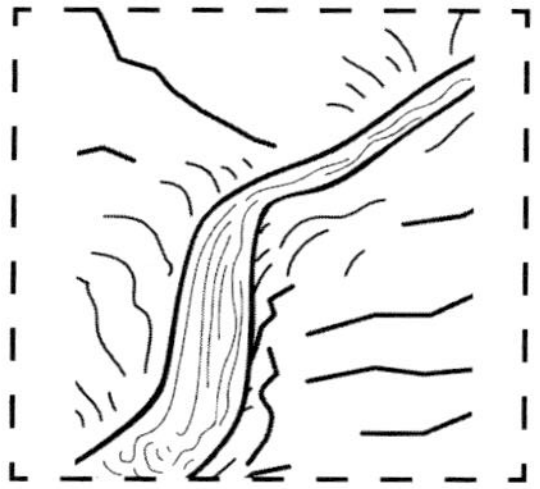

Word bank: river source; meanders; rapids; gorge; mouth; estuary; flood plain; waterfall; small stream

72   FOLENS GEOGRAPHY IN ACTION 6   © Folens (copiable page)

Information stream (1)

- Cut out and join this section of stream with the section on R10. Draw a map of the stream on A3 paper, then name the features in and around the stream, land uses, vegetation and the depth and speed of water flow using arrows of different thickness.

JOIN

10m
16 seconds

10m
26 seconds

10m
20 seconds

10m
23 seconds

© Folens (copiable page)   FOLENS GEOGRAPHY IN ACTION 6   73

Information stream (2)

(The boxes show depth of stream and speed of water.)

R10

JOIN

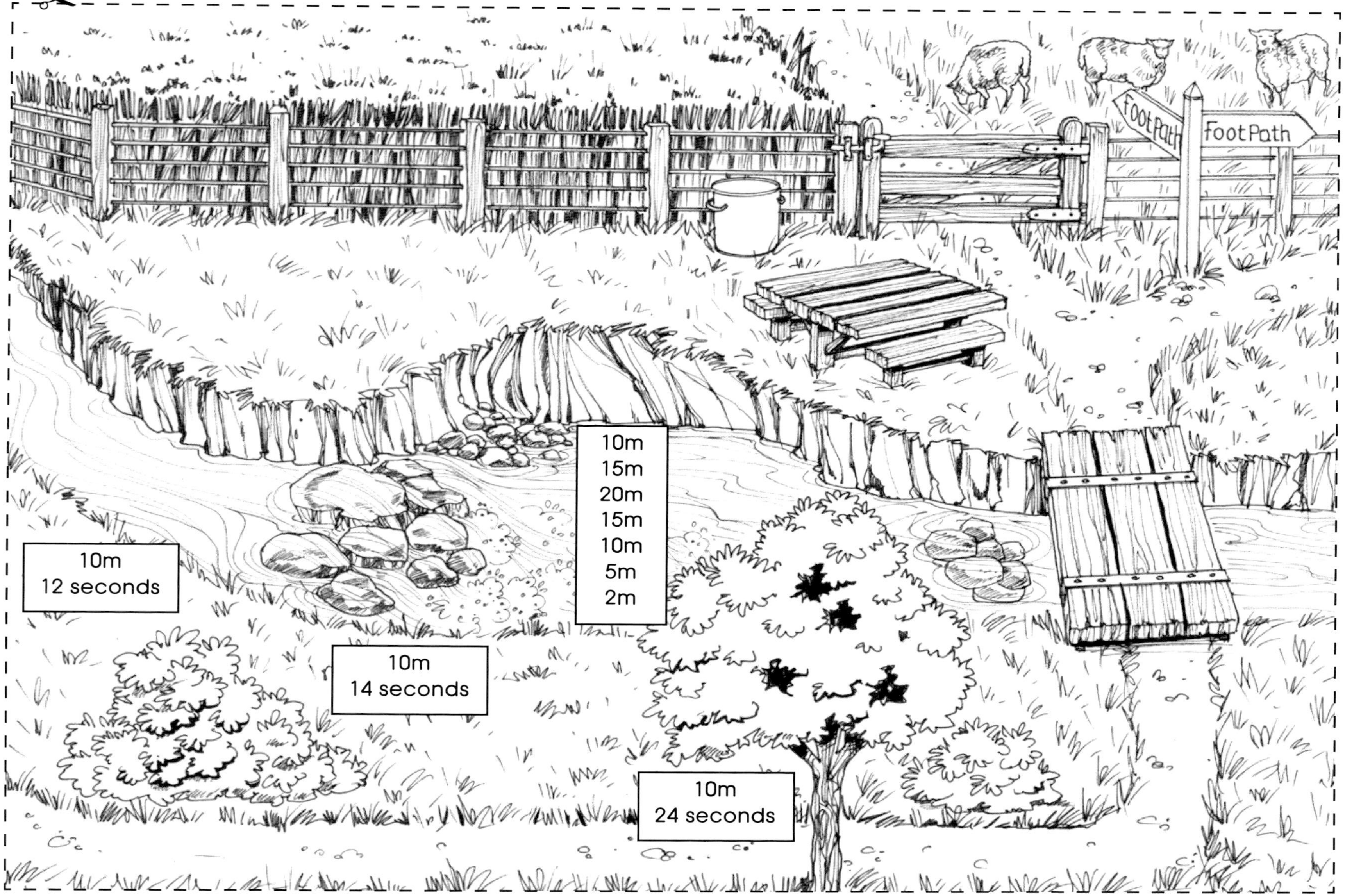

- 10m / 12 seconds
- 10m / 14 seconds
- 10m, 15m, 20m, 15m, 10m, 5m, 2m
- 10m / 24 seconds

Mapping streams

- Draw in the rivers and streams along the valley on map A.
- Draw in the pattern of contour lines you may find on an OS map on map B.

Map A

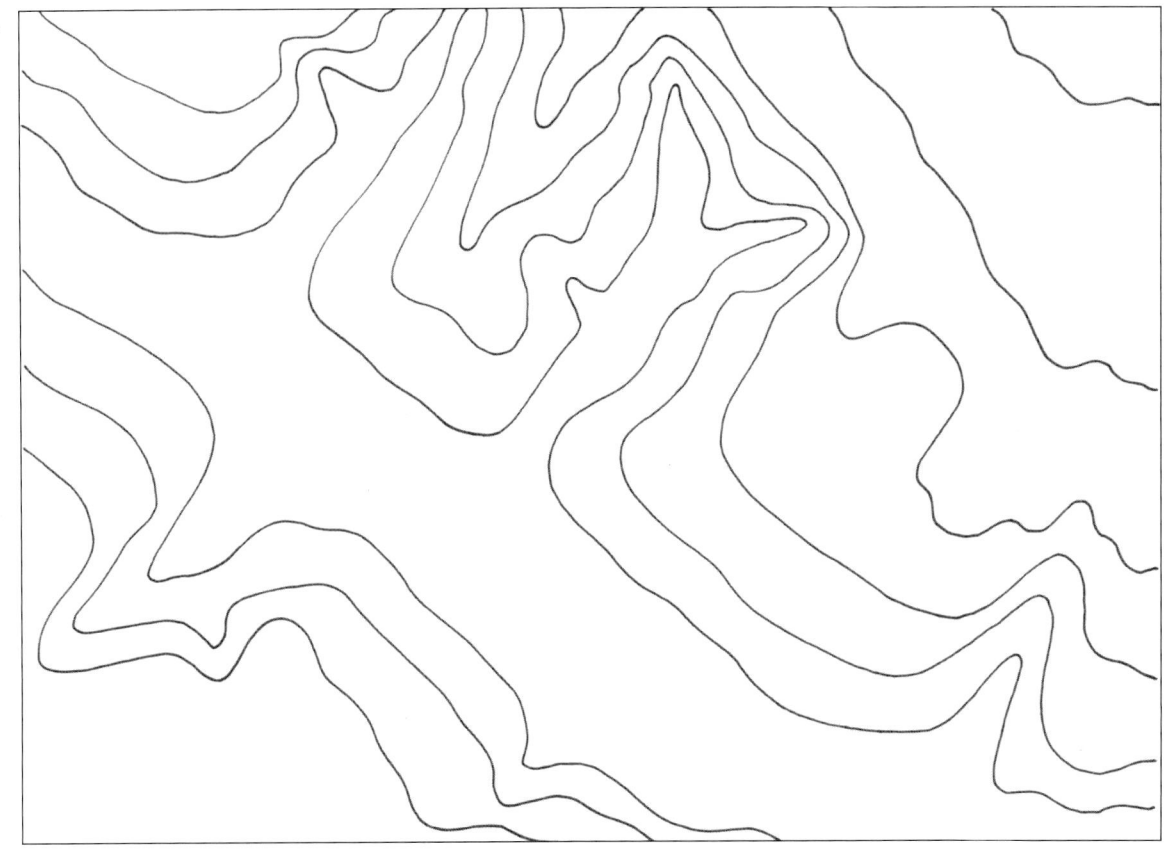

Map B

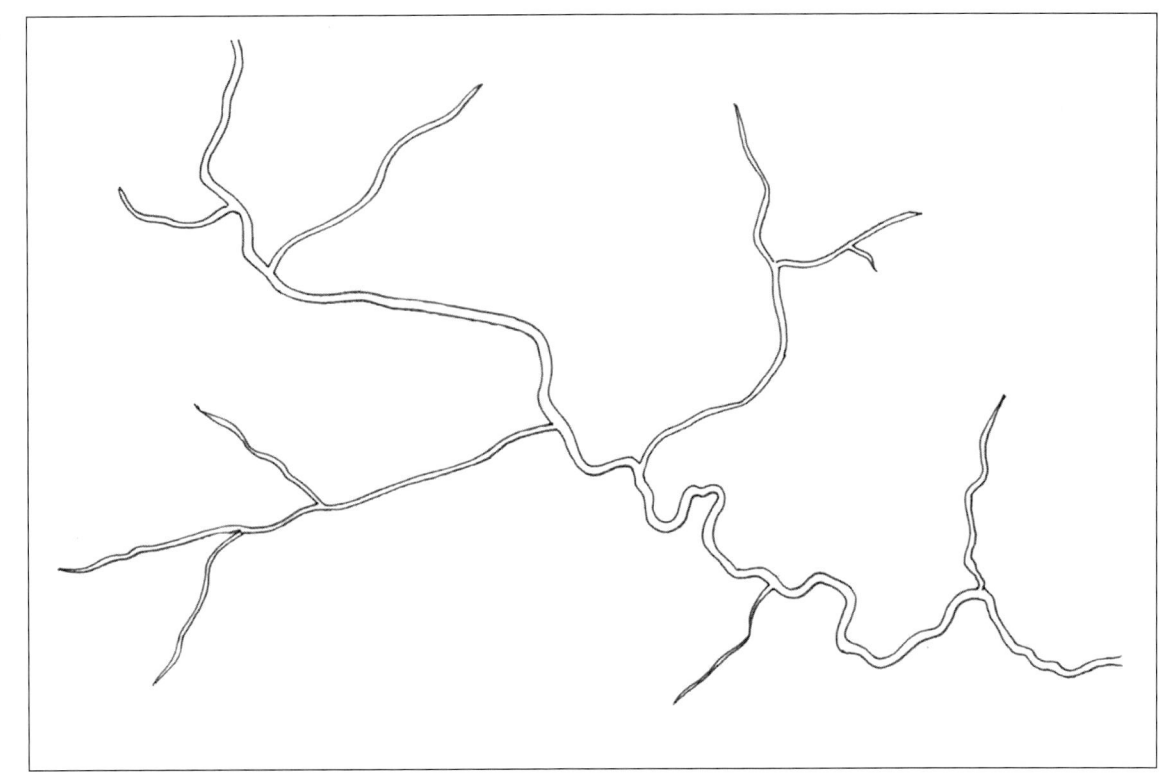

Key 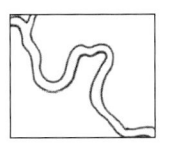 — river — contour line

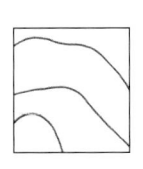

Rivers Near and Far

Learning Objectives

Children should:
- learn to use secondary sources including atlases, globes and ICT to investigate places
- learn about river systems and consider their environmental impact.

Background

This is an opportunity for children to gather information about rivers around the world and use a variety of resources. Reference materials should include books, a selection of different atlases, globes, photographs, newspapers, magazine articles, CD-ROMs and the Internet.

Starting Points	Main Activity	Simplified Activity	Extension Activity
R12 *'River file'* Look at maps of the UK and talk about the rivers. Follow the course of a nearby river, identifying its source, the places that it flows through and the sea it flows into.	Ask the children, in pairs, to use a variety of atlases to gather information about some of the UK's most important rivers and then complete a file for each one.	Ask the children to find out the names of all the rivers shown and then complete files for one or two rivers that are close to school.	Ask the children to look at atlas maps of the UK and to plot the course of other UK rivers not shown on the activity sheet.
R13 *'Flood'* Talk about why rivers flood and the floodplain along the sides of the lower reaches of a river, across which the river floods during periods of prolonged heavy rain. Talk about the folly of building houses on floodplains.	Ask the children to look at the location of the different settlements, the shape of the river and the dotted line which shows the limit of flooding. They should colour the rivers and streams dark blue, and the area of flood, light blue. They should consider the effect the flood will have on local people.	Together, look at the activity sheet and think about the area of land that will be flooded. List the buildings and areas of land that will be affected. Next to each, ask the children to note the damage that may occur and who will be most affected.	Ask the children to think of different ways to reduce the risk of flooding and damage to property that usually follows. Ask them to research flood prevention schemes.
R14 and **R15** *'World rivers (1) and (2)'* These activity sheets are formats for the children to complete that will structure their project work on a river.	Together, look at all of the information that the children should include on the activity sheets.	Give the children a smaller range of reference materials that they will find useful for a particular river and complete some of the more difficult material for them.	Ask the children to plot some of the most important rivers in the world on an outline map. They should name each one and note the country it flows from and the sea or ocean it flows into.

Plenary

Ask individual children to talk to the rest of the class about the rivers they have studied in the UK or elsewhere in the world. Display the children's river study sheets in a ring binder or on the wall linked to maps of the UK, Europe and the world.

River file

- Using a variety of atlases, label the rivers shown on the map. Research and complete a factfile for each of the rivers using index cards. First, complete the one below.

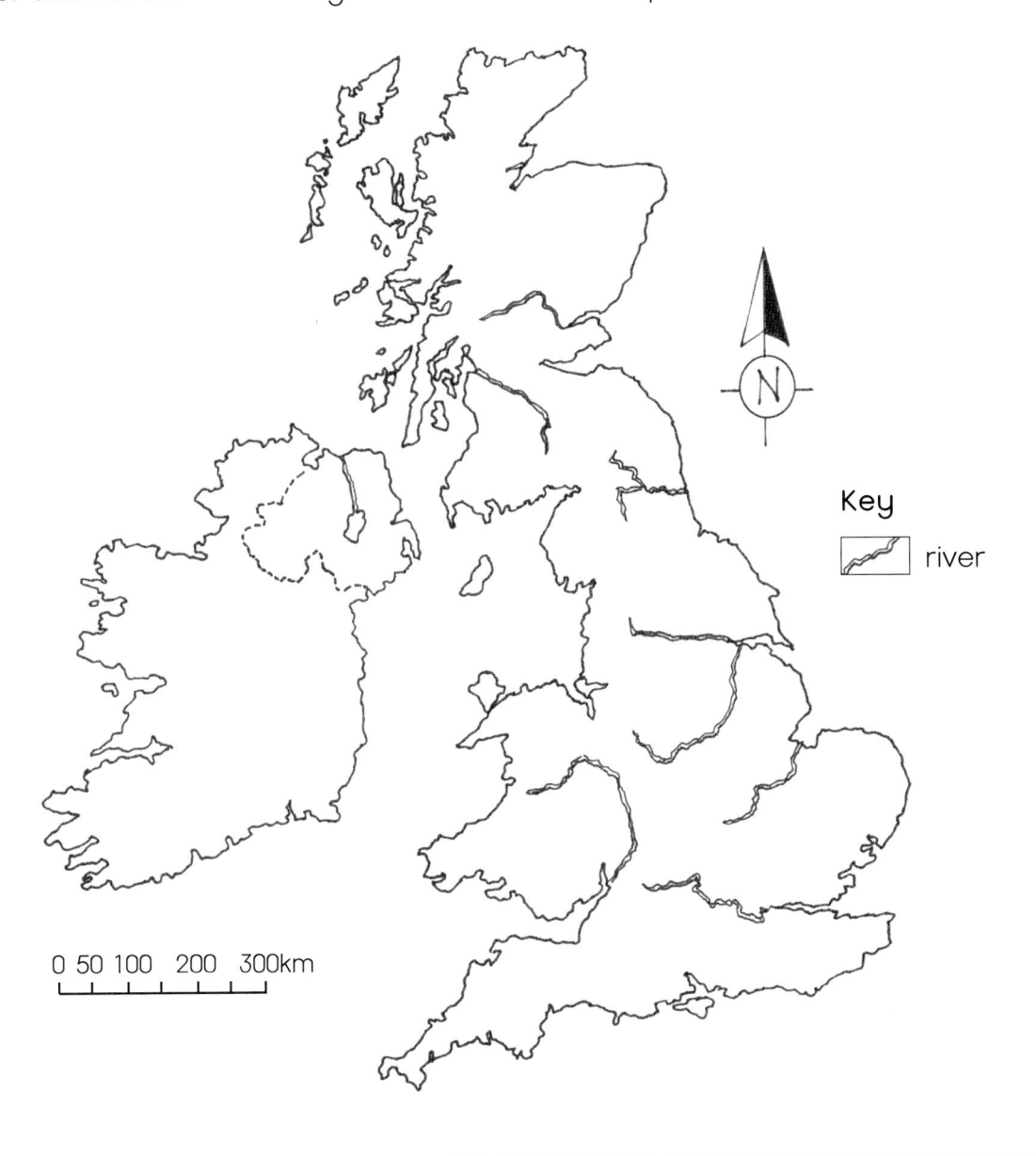

Key

river

0 50 100 200 300km

River file

Name _____

Source _____

Direction(s) of flow _____

Distance from the sea _____

Sea it flows into _____

Towns it passes through _____

Flood

R13

- Colour the river and streams dark blue, and the area up to the limit of flooding, light blue. Write about who will be affected when the river floods.

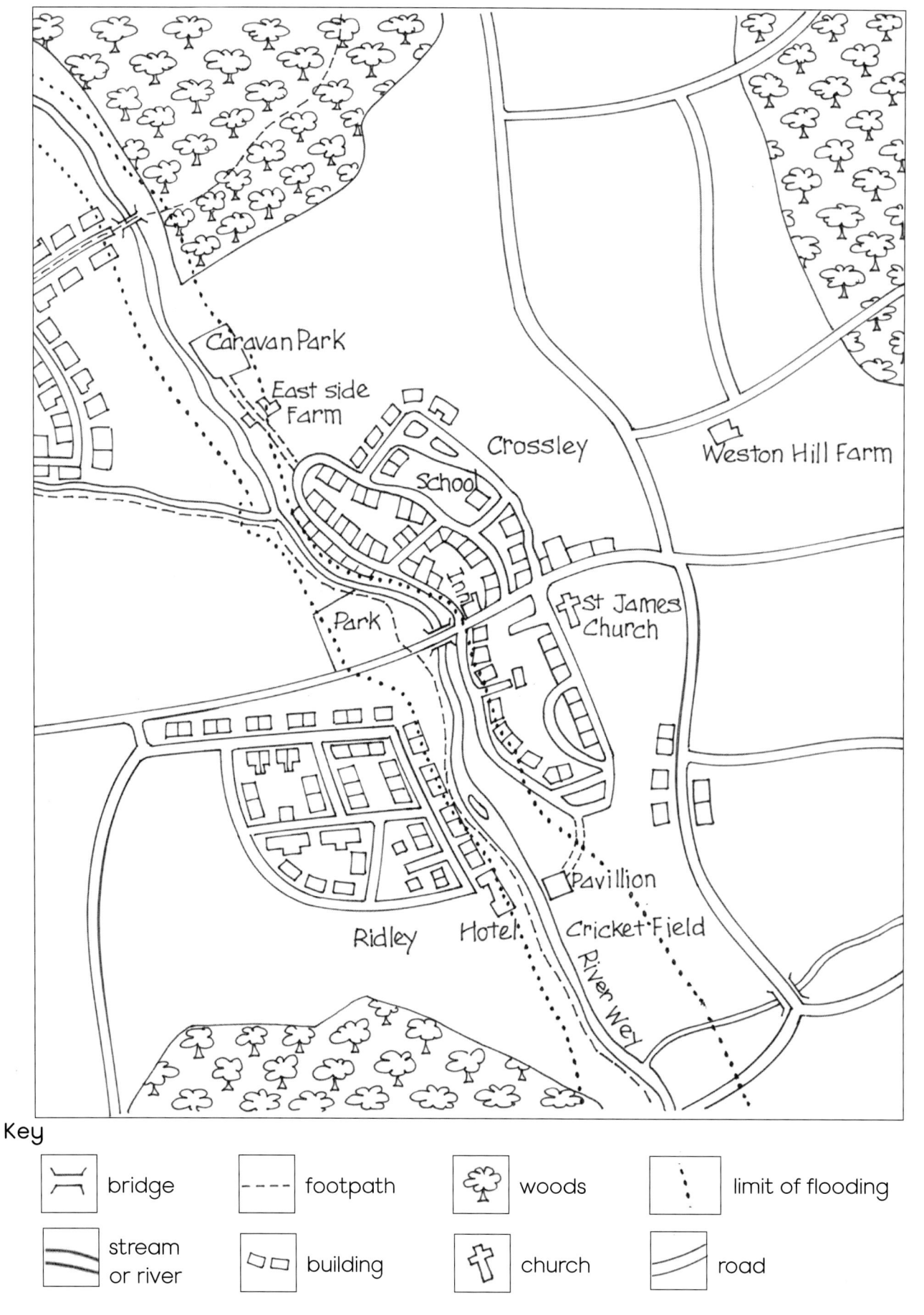

Labels on map: Caravan Park, East side Farm, Crossley, School, Weston Hill Farm, Park, St James Church, Ridley, Hotel, Pavillion, Cricket Field, River Wey

Key

bridge	bridge
- - - -	footpath
woods	woods
⋮	limit of flooding
stream or river	stream or river
▭▭	building
✝	church
road	road

78   FOLENS GEOGRAPHY IN ACTION 6   © Folens (copiable page)

World rivers (1)

R14

- Choose a river to study. Collect information about it and complete the table below.

River's name –
Map of the river –

River's source –	Towns and cities the river flows through –
	SOURCE ↓
Direction(s) it flows in –	
Length of the river –	
Sea it flows into –	
Distance from the UK (London) –	

World rivers (2)

- Choose a river to study. Collect information about it and complete the table below.

Human activity, industry/farming along the river –

Downloaded image from the Internet –

River features, history, beliefs –

Sketch of a cross-section of the river –